WHEN YOUR
CHILD
IS BEING BULLIED

REAL
SOLUTIONS
FOR PARENTS, EDUCATORS &
OTHER PROFESSIONALS

WHEN YOUR
CHILD
IS BEING BULLIED

REAL
SOLUTIONS
FOR PARENTS, EDUCATORS &
OTHER PROFESSIONALS

J.E. DiMARCO & M.K. NEWMAN

ISBN 13: 978-1-58776-181-2

Library of Congress Number: 2011927613

Author Photos: Photo by mattferguson.com

Manufactured in the United States of America

VIVISPHERE
PUBLISHING

675 Dutchess Turnpike, Poughkeepsie, NY 12603
www.vivisphere.com (800) 724-1100

SPECIAL THANKS AND LOTS OF LOVE TO:

Our husbands, whose amazing love, strength and support made this project possible.

Our children, who teach us new things every day about resilience, optimism,
love, compassion, empathy and respect.

Our parents and siblings, who helped us become who we are today and taught us to do
the right thing, even when it was the most difficult and most unpopular thing to do.

All our friends, who were there for us in thick, thin and everything in between.

The Law offices of Katten Muchin Rosenman, LLP for their expertise,
counsel, support and generosity.

CONTENTS

FOREWORD

This book is precisely what many parents ask for when I am touring the country raising awareness about the devastation that results from bullying. While there are many experts and advocates that can tell you how to prevent bullying or how pervasive it is, there are not any manuals on how to stop your child's torment at the hands of a bully and get back to happiness.

Until you are a parent of a bullied child, it is hard to imagine the humiliation, frustration and utter sadness bullying brings on a child as well as the child's family. Not only do the authors understand this issue, they lived it.

Whenever I need a recommendation on anything, I find someone who has experienced it and had great success. The authors of "When Your Child Is Being Bullied: Real Solutions" is that someone you should turn to for answers.

The following pages will walk you through how to solve your child's issues in an easy to understand and practical way.

My best to you and your families,

John Halligan
Ryan's Story
Ryanpatrickhalligan.org

INTRODUCTION

The majority of parents with children who have been bullied for an extended length of time tell us that the bully stole their son's or daughter's childhood.

After experiencing the tragedy of bullying with our own children, and finding a way back to happiness, we felt we needed to offer some solutions to others facing the same situation.

Time not only heals all wounds, it also provides clarity and perspective. We started writing this book with the goal of providing families with a systematic guide to stop their children's torment and get beyond the challenges. What we did not know was that many other interested parties were looking for a similar resource. While we were conducting research and meeting with experts, parents, and schools, we learned that educators, therapists, pediatricians, social workers, community leaders, and faith leaders were also interested in using the same information and recommendations.

To that end, it is our sincere hope that this manual will help anyone who wants to eliminate any and all types of bullying for a child, and help them get back to just being a child.

Chapter One
Our Stories:
We Understand Your
Frustration

Believe us when we say we understand how frustrating it is to try and solve your child's victimization when he is being bullied. We really do. We lived it. We made mistakes and we succeeded in stopping the bullying and restoring happiness in our children's lives against some pretty big odds.

Our families' stories are shared here to help other families learn how to avoid key mistakes along the journey to stop the bullying and get beyond a child's torment.

There are 25 million families in the U.S. today with similar stories. If you take nothing else away from our book, please know:

- *There are solutions that work and will move you beyond the torment.*
- *You are not alone.*

At the end of both stories, we list our "lessons learned" as a result of our experiences. Lessons learned will be shared at the end of each chapter and will hopefully help each of you.

THE NEWMAN FAMILY STORY

Our bullying story begins when my son, Tim, was in fifth grade. Tim is very bright, kind, a bit sensitive, and a rule-follower. The bullying played out over about 18 months. At the end of this time, we had a happy ending with a dramatic and very effective solution, but it was challenging getting there. Know this: happy endings happen all the time!

Tim was taunted for all the same reasons every child is teased. Typically, boys in fourth and fifth grade like to do things, such as repeating something over and over again,

1

until the taunted child gets very upset. Even when a child sees the other upset, 10 and 11 year old boys have trouble stopping. We were forgiving of this type of behavior even though it was frequent. My husband and I thought it was truly benign and felt our son should simply ignore it.

Other motivations for taunting Tim stemmed from the fact that he was well liked by teachers because he was respectful and worked hard. This irritated "beginner bullies" in the class because it made them look and feel less important in some way.

Frequently, between the ages of 10 and 11 years old, all children have a hard time making small talk and revert to teasing to get attention and "fill dead air." Other common things children do at these ages is to mock others in a voice resembling someone who is developmentally or speech challenged. A few boys mocked Tim in this way on a regular basis. In another common event, children would talk about embarrassing events from earlier grades, embellish them and retell the story over and over. Note: up until this point I never refer to any of this as bullying because my husband and I viewed it as immaturity and teasing. This picked up steam in fifth grade, but it was nothing like what was to come in sixth grade. Tim finished fifth grade with some wounds to his ego from the excessive teasing, but he seemed to manage it well. He felt like sixth grade was going to be a great fresh start. Unfortunately, he was quite wrong.

Tim's first few weeks at middle school went without incident, we thought. Then, it all started. My husband and I had no idea he was being ridiculed constantly for the first month and a half. We actually were feeling good. Further, almost foolishly, we would say things like, "He seems really happy" and "Tim is very big and strong. He is a very capable defensive lineman on the football team, nobody would want to mess around with him." Wrong. They may not have physically tormented him (they would not be so obvious or foolish); instead, the sixth grade bullies had a much worse plan than physically bullying. It is called *full and utter humiliation*. Constantly.

At this point you are probably asking yourself, "Why Tim?" We have many theories. Tim did not fit in a specific bucket in sixth grade. He was not a super-athlete. He was not a *cool kid*. He was not super popular. He is very smart and a good football player as well as being a good musician. Most of all, Tim is kind, respectful, empathetic, and a thinker above all else.

In answer to the question, the real reason was not simple. We believe very popular children tend to capriciously target less popular children and make them feel lowly so they can feel better about themselves. As we now know, the reasons can be unclear and completely random. In a couple of situations, there was a sense that certain bully children were jealous and had some level of anger management issues. We will never know for sure.

In any event, after the first few weeks of school, Tim did share a few events that seemed excessive and mean. We chalked it up to *middle school stuff*. These events included several boys telling him he was bad at sports, pushing books out of his hands, and asking him humiliating and demeaning questions. While we felt that was very mean, it only got worse.

At lunch, certain groups told him "he was not allowed here." Sometimes, others defended him, but with little success most of the time. What we did not know is that a few of the primary bullies had recruited other bullies to taunt Tim. Further, in the first month or two of school the primary bullies had shared some of Tim's more embarrassing moments from third and fourth grade with new classmates from feeder elementary schools, and, worse, embellished the stories to the point where they became humiliating for Tim. By month two of middle school, the rumor mill was wide and deep about Tim. We had no idea that in the first six weeks at a new school, a few very cruel children had ruined Tim's reputation.

As you can imagine, these stories spread like wildfire and suddenly sixth graders, both boys and girls, began coming up to Tim on a daily basis and taunting him with stories about his former years. It got to the point that Tim had one major source of bullying in almost every class.

Over the coming weeks, Tim got a little quieter, and, clearly, a little more frustrated. He began looking down a lot and avoiding eye contact. By the second week of November, he could not take it anymore. On the morning of one of his football playoff games, he shared something with us that still haunts me. On a day that should have been very joyful, he was overcome with pain over constant bullying. Tim's team was a powerhouse. They were headed toward another championship, and he should have been completely charged and excited, but he was not.

Instead, as my husband and I read the Saturday morning newspaper, Tim came in upset and blurted out, "I have been lying to you." We asked about what. He answered with big tears, "Everybody hates me and makes fun of me, and nobody respects me." Oh, God, I was stabbed right in my heart. Those words killed me in a nanosecond. All I could think is, "its back." I thought this nonsense was over, and it was not.

Tim started with, "…somehow everybody knows stuff about me that is embarrassing. People are calling me terrible names and some of the names don't even make sense." I will not share the specific names that he was called, but they were all expletive ridden and ranged from being mentally incompetent, to being inadequate at athletics, to being a loser, and worse. You can guess how hurtful many of the names were. As a side note, all of these incidents are considered harassment, and, because they were frequent, we now know these events were actually criminal, and charges could have been pressed against these families. We learned this much later.

Tim indicated that the hallways, gym class, and, before/after school were the worst. Even a few classrooms were filled with horror for him. We asked him about his friends. He was still doing things on a regular basis and all seemed normal with them. Tim indicated his friends were treating him well, but really could not defend him, because then they would be tortured too. He was right.

After he shared all of the details of what he had been through for the last two months, he offered a solution to us that still makes me cry when I think about it. He said, "I know what we can do. We can pretend I was in a horrible car accident and died. That way, I can come back in a few months as a new kid and nobody will bother me." My heart leapt into my throat. Somehow, we remained calm.

You can guess all of the questions we had following that statement. "Do you feel like you want to be in a car accident? Are you thinking about getting into a car accident or doing something that will hurt yourself?" After lots of discussion, we realized he was simply being a creative 11-year-old problem solver, and did not wish to hurt himself or others. We did keep a very close eye on his behavior; and, what he said and did from that point on.

This was the proverbial "straw that broke the camel's back." That was it. It was Saturday, but we put calls into the superintendent, the principal, and the counselor, and on and on.

On Monday morning, we had a meeting with everyone but the superintendent (in hindsight, we should have demanded she be included). In that meeting, we described the various, layered accounts of bullying my son was experiencing. We were very close to pulling Tim out of that school and moving him to a private school. I distinctly remember saying, "We cannot take on 13 families in this community. I have no idea what to do. I think we have to transfer him, his reputation has been completely ruined." At that point, they assured us that they could solve it. Concurrent to all of this, Tim was very worried about reporting the bullies because he knew there would be retaliation. He was absolutely right.

The principal, assistant principal, and counselor suggested rather than transferring Tim, that they could address each bully and get this nailed down. They were extremely apologetic and empathetic. After we reviewed the approach, my husband and I stated very clearly to the principal, "There must be a consequence for each child, because just asking them to stop bullying will not work with sixth grade boys!"

In this case, I get to say I-told-you-so very loudly. The assistant principal did speak to most of the 13 boys, but a few were not contacted. To be clear, there were no consequences for these children. This was a mistake. We'll discuss this more later. From there, many of the bullies stopped, but some of the bullies occasionally mocked Tim for tattling and all excluded him from activities. One of the primary bullies was on his winter sports team and continued to do rude things when others were not looking, particularly when adults were not present.

As the winter break approached, the bullying ramped up a bit, but Tim was loathing the thought of tattling again and receiving yet more retaliation. We spoke to the teachers, counselor, and assistant principal. They decided that addressing the gym class, and others as a group, and discussing the need for respect, was the best way to handle it. They did speak in groups with the children, but, unfortunately, it did not work.

After winter break, the bullying was less, but always there. Now, it had mostly transformed to exclusion tactics. While friends still supported Tim, it was challenging to meet new friends because of the constant gossip mill and bullying. Kids, who were not friendly with Tim, avoided him because they did not want to risk being bullied themselves, even if they liked Tim.

As February and March passed, it became clear the bullying was ramping up. I put a few calls into the principal and assistant principal. Some calls were not returned. The reason for this was the administrators had their hands full with many other bullying situations. Apparently, the bullying was everywhere, and they were struggling to get several situations under control. I was forgiving of the lack of attention because they seemed to be doing their best. In a few isolated instances, Tim's bullies were called into the office and reprimanded, but never with a consequence of any meaning, and only sometimes were the parents called.

Meanwhile, Tim met with the sixth grade counselor a few times. She had a few helpful ideas, but, unfortunately and unwittingly, gave Tim the worst advice possible. I say unwittingly, because there are very few counselors in the U.S. who are trained to effectively deal with bullying. Much of the old thinking does not really work. Tim was advised to "count how many times you can ignore it without reacting." Tim tried this, but it did not work. Several humiliating events occurred in the locker room and hallways. Some of them were quite disturbing. For the record, ignoring it does not work with hard-core bullying, it only fuels a bully to do it more.

The most humiliating event came in April on *his birthday*. I still get quite angry when I think about this. During a passing period between classes, a large group of bullies surrounded Tm and sang a children's song that was known to bug him. They taunted him. They embarrassed him. On his birthday! They would not let him out of the circle, so he pushed two of them down and walked away. They all laughed and retold the story to their friends. Weirdly, most kids thought this shameful event was actually funny.

When he got home, he shared this with me, and I was outraged. He was so frustrated. Of course being a mother, I went out and bought some additional birthday presents to make up for his despair. I took a couple of days to calm down, and tried to think clearly. At this time, I did not want Tim to receive more retaliation, so I was debating whether to report it or not. I was at lunch with a good friend a few days later and she made me realize that I needed to make a stink about this right away.

The next day, I called the assistant principal. He really was a great advocate for Tim, but he simply did not have the policies or protocol in place to combat this type of prolonged and strategic bullying. The assistant principal was being challenged with several other bullying situations where the current policies only worked some of the time. He was frustrated too.

When we spoke about what had happened on Tim's birthday, he agreed this was not acceptable, and that it would be addressed. Again, all but a few of the bullies were brought in and threatened with suspension. I drafted a letter that was designed to require that each child cease and desist all bullying, outlining the specific behaviors that must stop. The assistant principal sent the letter home and required signatures from parents. Each parent was spoken to directly.

This is the kicker. Of those 13 or so kids that were addressed in the assistant principal's office, not one family called us to apologize or even acknowledge this occurred. My husband and I were incredulous. This cannot be. If our kids had done this and we were called, we would have personally delivered an apology alongside our child. In addition, there would have been a major consequence for our child. We will talk much more about this in other chapters.

Prior to this, I had begun quite a bit of research on bullying. At the same time, a good friend of mine whose child was a year younger and who was being cyber-bullied, was doing some research as well. We read extensively on the topic, and called on experts for advice. We also reviewed all of the legal and law enforcement options available to us in this situation.

After the birthday incident and the attempt to address it, the bullying did stop, but now Tim was largely ignored by many classmates and pegged as a "narc", or informant. He was basically a pariah. Friends of his were supportive, but did not buck the bullies. At this point, I decided rather than continue to complain about this issue in our school district, I would get it out in the open and fix it. After all, we really do believe most bullies (not all, but most) can be reformed.

My good friend, and co-author, and I did just that. We put a team of experts together, and completed a full secondary research study, as well as a best practices study. From there, we built a presentation including tactics and recommendations, and met with the superintendent, school board and principals. The final chapter of our story is dedicated to providing step-by-step instructions on how to start an anti-bullying program in schools.

Simultaneous to all of that, my friend and I decided to talk more openly about our children and their victimization. We received many phone calls from families in the same bullying boat. After that, summer came, and so did park district summer camps. A few of the primary bullies chose to start in again at various camps. Tim quit the camps.

I made overtures to the parents of bullies as a means to include them in our district wide efforts to solve the bullying problem. A "no" response was received. These people have no accountability, no remorse. Amazing. I still scratch my head at this.

Tim went to the first week of seventh grade football camp on the first day of August. Football, in the town we lived in at that time, was like football in Texas. It is a big deal. The tackle football program starts in third grade. The program is five days a week for two hours a day. Each practice involves hard workouts and skills training. This was Tim's third year. He had trained quite a bit and was ready. His self-confidence was great going into camp. He was incredibly excited!

Unfortunately, a group of bullies chose to humiliate Tim the first night of practice. He ignored it and despite them, had a great performance on the field. The coaches were impressed.

When Tim came home, he was very upset and told us how he had been humiliated. We called all of the parents of those children that taunted him that night, including the primary bully who started all of this nonsense 18 months prior. We were, and still are, incredulous at the level of obsession this primary bully had for Tim.

About 20% of these parents were apologetic. A few were nonplussed. The entire football league was notified. The bullying episodes stopped and were nonexistent during the season, throughout the league. The coaches all jumped on this issue, and bullying was vanquished inside the football program.

We started to review new school options for Tim. We toured several. Tim maintained that this bullying was over, and asked, "Why should I have to leave the school that I love. The bullies should have to leave." We could not find a great private school, so we decided to give it one more chance at his middle school, and he went back again.

The final event that changed everything was on the first day of school that year. While Tim's classmates at his seventh grade level behaved well and treated him with respect, others in grades below and above had been recruited to taunt him. The new bully recruits worked on him all day long on the first day. That was *really* it. Yet, again, there was another series of calls with principals and unapologetic parents. We knew this school was not meant to be.

We knew we had to take a big step and, while we began to figure it out, Tim went to school the next day. In his very first passing period, he got taunted. He tossed this unwitting child (this child was a pawn and had been put up to it by another bully) up against the lockers like a rag doll. A teacher stopped it, and handled it well as he was aware of Tim's situation.

I picked Tim up at 9:00 a.m. on that day, and he has not been back to that school since then. We withdrew him from the public middle school, and enrolled him in a new private school that is wonderful. He thrived academically, emotionally, and socially. The children at his new school were fun, happy, loud, sometimes even obnoxious, but always acted with respect and were always supportive and caring. What a difference.

This is an important message: most kids are respectful, empathetic and caring. And, the good news is, they are everywhere. The lesson learned is that the issue was not with my son. He clearly was fine once he was in a healthy environment. When he was in the unhealthy environment, he did not do well. We should have changed schools sooner. There can be happy endings. However, getting there is sometimes circuitous and extremely challenging. Transferring is not the only solution. There are many others. Read on.

LESSONS LEARNED

- Bullies select targets capriciously. There is seldom a real reason why a victim is selected. Remember, bullying is abnormal social behavior, and is never invited or deserved.

- Once you identify that the behavior is bullying, do not ignore it. Ignoring it is only effective with light teasing, not bullying. Information is included to help a parent discern the difference between basic teasing and bulling.

- Insulate your child when they are going to a new school or going into the upper elementary grades:

    o Make sure your child has a few solid friends.

    o Make sure your child knows a few older, respectful, and helpful kids who can watch out for them at school and protect them.

    o If your child walks to school, make sure he/she has a team of supportive kids to walk with everyday.

- Either make sure the school administrator, or you, call the parents of the bully once your child has identified the individual.

- In order to avoid retaliation, make sure that it is clear once the bully has been reprimanded that he/she promises there will be no further retaliation. If they do retaliate or talk about the event/reprimand, they will receive a consequence.

- Make certain there is some form of consequence after the first event.

- Confirm that all bullies who played a role in each event are addressed.

- If there is a group of bullies, get to the ringleader and squelch the source. This will be discussed further.

The DiMarco Family

I am the mother of two boys–two very different boys. My younger son is very out-going, uninhibited, and enjoys having a magnitude of friends. He views school as more of a social event than a place to get a formal education. My older son is a boy of few words. He is a bit introverted, always follows the rules, loves to read, and has a few select friends. School for him is a place where you study and learn, not a place to just have fun.

A child started bullying my oldest son in the first grade. Although I really did not think it was bullying at the time. I recall my son telling me about a friend of a friend who was mean to him at recess–calling my son names, teasing him, and excluding him from games. The so-called usual kid stuff. My husband recited the line "boys will be boys", and we left it at that. After a few more "boys will be boys" incidents, my husband told our son to toughen up, and stand up for himself. I decided to step in when my husband suggested to our son to "just sock him one". That was what my husband did in his day, which seemed to rectify a situation quickly. I reminded my husband that the *zero tolerance for violence* policy at our school, and a punch, would get our son suspended. At the time, our school did not have a forceful bully policy so boy stuff on the playground was not a punishable offense.

My husband and I had many conversations about what to do. We definitely dis-agreed on what exactly is bullying and how to handle it. My husband came from a family of seven siblings, four of them boys. If he did not stand up for himself, being one of the youngest brothers, his life was going to be filled with torment. I was the youngest of three girls. Pulling hair and taking each other's sweaters was the extent of our issues, but, be-cause I had been bullied myself, I was very sensitive to the matter. My husband's plan of socking him one was not going to solve the problem, not to mention it would get our son in a heap of trouble. So, we suggested that he just ignore this child. Little did we know that ignoring the kid would just fuel the bully's fire. You will hear this frequently. However, do not ignore bullying; it only makes it worse.

It was not until the fourth grade that I realized the bullying had gone on far too long. Our very serious student did not want to go to school. He often complained of a head-ache; the next day a stomachache; the following day a sore throat; and so on. It took several days for me to catch on. I knew something was bothering him, but I just could not figure out what it was. Other odd things happened, such as every time the phone rang, he jumped a foot. If the doorbell rang, he would run to his room. He did not want to do anything socially, including having his best buddy over to hang out with him. He began sleeping more than usual, eating often, and he just seemed unhappy. I never guessed he was being bullied, let alone being "cyber bullied" since we prohibited him from using the computer for recreation. The rule in our house was that the boys could use the computer for homework and only as long as an adult was supervising.

The clue that led me to figure out what was going on with him was the day I walked into the kitchen, and he abruptly slammed the laptop closed. He had a petrified look on his face. He did not look like he was doing something wrong, but it was more like he did not want me to know something. The look only a mother can read. I did not approach him at the time except to remind him of the computer use rule. I knew he was not going to fess up, but I knew I was closer to figuring it out.

After he went to bed that night, I looked at the history on the computer. I saw that he had been looking at YouTube. It appeared that he disobeyed our strict rule about the computer and opened a YouTube account. I was amazed he even knew how to sign up for an account. Yet, in all the chaos, he forgot to logout leading me to discover the "I hate DiMarco" channel. I clicked on the link, and, to my horrifying surprise, there were endless nasty statements written about my son–he is fat, stupid, and a bad football player–all of which were far from true. I immediately thought, "Who the [heck] would write such horrible things about my son?"

At first, I was unable to find the source of who was writing these things because the profile of the perpetrator stated he was a 35-year-old man–I became afraid. Was an older man harassing my son, or God forbid, was he being abused by someone? As I poked around further, I found videos created by this person. It turned out it was a boy from his grade. The same boy who was calling him names many years ago at recess. I had to stop and ask myself if I had let the "boys will be boys" theme go on for way too long. The truth is, I did. Despite the disagreement I had with my husband on the precise definition of bullying, it was time to do something about it immediately.

My first step was to do some research on bullying. I wanted to make sure this was nipped in the bud as soon as possible. I was very disappointed that I had not reacted sooner. My son was trying to tell me about the situations in the past, but I had not picked up on it. After discussing it with my husband, we decided the best thing to do was to find out what other parents have done in these situations. I did not find much written by parents except for a blog entry or two, but what I did find were some articles and websites dedicated to bullying. I spent several hours searching through everything I could find and came up with a plan.

My second step was to talk to our son, although I knew that was not going to be easy since he was not saying much. I had remembered watching an episode of Oprah while I was in the hospital on bed rest during my pregnancy with my second son. There was an expert on her show discussing how to connect with your kids, specifically how to get through to boys. I remember this person saying that you can get a boy to talk more if he is doing one of his favorite activities. That is what I did. We decided to take his best friend, a 140-pound Alaskan malamute, for a walk. At first, we did not talk much at all, and then I just started asking questions, mostly general questions about school, football, and friends. Slowly, he started to give me hints about what was going on at school and on YouTube. I asked him how he felt about it, and he eventually revealed that was the source of his unhappiness. My impatience thickened at the slow rate of details I was receiving regarding the situation. I quickly started firing away questions and becoming visibly upset. Unfortunately, this led me to disciplining him for not following the rules on the computer. Perhaps, I should have left my "I told you so" attitude for my next discussion I had with my husband, rather than making a bad situation worse with my son. To my disappointment, my son quickly clammed up and that was the end of any disclosed details. My son did not want me to do anything, yet I knew something had to be done.

My third step was to contact the parents of the child who was harassing my son. Since this was somewhat of a minor incident, I did not want to make the situation worse for my son. I wanted to avoid having a retaliation that could be potentially more detrimental than the situation at hand. The parents were not home, so I left a message explaining the situation. I stated, "Our boys don't have to be friends; however, I don't want them to be disrespectful to each other either". I did not receive a call back, so I called again. This time I requested that the "I hate DiMarco" page be removed. I gave it a couple of days, and when that did not happen, I decided to call the school to see if they could be of some assistance.

My first call was to the principal. I explained to her the circumstances. She found it hard to believe that a group of fourth graders was cyber bullying. After all, this was something you see at the middle school level. The principal tried to be helpful. However, she felt because it was not on school property, it was not a school issue. As an aside, we now know that in most states, the school is still obligated to help when students are involved. I then called the fourth grade teacher and explained the situation to her. She did confirm that my son was acting unusually quiet, and that he did not want to participate in recess. The teacher had witnessed a few comments made by some kids to my son, but because my son did not seem upset about it at the time, she dismissed it. The teacher decided it was best to bring my son and the other child together to discuss the situation and explain that this behavior is considered bullying. That seemed to do the trick. The "I hate DiMarco" page was been taken down. However, much to the teacher's disappointment, an "I hate Sally" page was posted in its place.

The bully had moved on to someone else. This time the bully had recruited more kids, really good kids, and instructed them to write nasty things about Sally. Sally was the new target. Sally's parents were a lot less patient than I was. They went immediately to the principal, called all the parents involved, and e-mailed all the parents in the class about the situation. Many kids were disciplined this time around. I admit, I think Sally's parents approach was much more effective.

My last step was to work with my son on sticking up for himself. Research shows children who are more non-confrontational and quieter than other children, are often bullied more than those who exhibit greater self-confidence. I did some role-playing with my son and discussed how to handle certain situations. I tried to explain that while most people are good people, unfortunately, some people can be mean, and it is important not to "get walked on." He is such a good-hearted kid that it was difficult for him to accept this. It is one of the lessons in life he had to learn at a very early age. My goal was to give him the tools and words to use should he ever be in a situation like that again. Although he still gets petty harassment from the kids from time to time, it is much more tame such as mocking, talking to him in a childish voice, or rumors about his athletic ability. His fifth grade teacher did call me to inform me about a few situations and to let me know that he had addressed them with the bully. I am grateful to have such a respectable teacher looking out for him.

I truly believe it is extremely important to stop a bullying problem immediately, before it escalates. Since I was severely bullied as a child, I can say, "I know how you are feeling", because it is hurtful. The old saying of "sticks and stones" needs revision to read, "Sticks and stones may break my bones but names will hurt me too!"

LESSONS LEARNED

- Do not ignore the signs of bullying.
- Ask for help from teachers, coaches, principals and counselors.
- Do not assume it is "kid stuff" or "boys will be boys; girls will be girls".
- Use child safety software on all your computers and do not allow your child to use Facebook, YouTube, MySpace or other types of social media without adult supervision.
- If your child is severely bullied, consider getting professional help.
- Do not let your child's full potential be hindered because of a bully.
- Help your child regain confidence and self-esteem.

Chapter Two
The Bullying Heartbreak

S ome parents, adults and children may say the word "epidemic" is an exaggeration when speaking about bullying in the U.S. It is not an exaggeration. By definition, bullying *is* an epidemic today in the U.S. An epidemic is "a contagious disease spreading rapidly in an area." Bullying *is* a disease. It causes immediate pain and has symptoms. Most studies indicate that one out of every three to four children ages 10 to 15 years are bullied, moderately or severely, right now. Similarly, once it starts in a school or a community, it commonly spreads quickly and becomes a culturally accepted perspective across all socioeconomic levels.

Other unsettling statistics about this epidemic include:

- Each day 160,000 children miss school due to bullying in the U.S.

- At least 43% of middle school children avoid the bathroom and locker rooms at all costs due to the certainty of being bullied.

- The number one reason for suicides among children ages 11 to 15 is bullying.

- In the 1980s, the U.S. was ranked ninth among advanced nations on average across science, math and reading scores. The U.S. is now ranked 23rd according to "Waiting for Superman" directed by Davis Guggenheim, 2010.

Therefore, in purist terms, bullying in the U.S. has epidemic qualities based on its pervasiveness and negative effects, but truly has not been addressed with widespread solutions. This is largely due to the fact that changing attitudes and perspectives is actually significantly harder than developing treatments for physiological illnesses. Like an infectious disease, bullying is truly hard to control and even harder to find the source of the infection. In the case of bullying, finding the source can be a needle in the proverbial haystack because it is simply culturally accepted in many schools and communities as a way of life. That said, there are definitely some schools and communities who have had success with prevention, remediation and management of bullying. There are reasons to be hopeful with this epidemic.

WHAT IS THE DEFINITION OF BULLYING?

In order to answer completely why bullying is an epidemic, it is first important to define the term. It is interesting that many parents and school leaders claim bullying is extremely hard to define and manage. We might agree with the latter because anytime you are attempting to determine what is the best course to manage issues with kids, it is chal-lenging. It typically needs to be highly individualized on a case-by-case level and, of course, it takes time. However, we disagree that it is hard to define. We have found that many parents and school leaders actually want bullying to be hard to define because it is difficult to manage bullying. By making it seem as though it is very challenging to define, schools and communities are allowed to throw up their hands and claim that there is no solution because it is too mercurial and insidious to define and solve. To which, we say "nonsense."

The following is a general hybrid definition many experts would agree upon. Bullying is an "Abusive behavior against a victim(s). It can be a direct attack such as teasing, taunting, threatening, stalking, name-calling, hitting, making threats, coercion and stealing, or more subtle through malicious gossiping, spreading rumors and intentional exclusion. All of which can be implemented in person, online or through electronics."

Most experts agree there are two key components to a bullying relationship that are always present:

1. *Bullies do not stop "teasing" when asked* by their victim, nor do they stop when the victim is obviously upset, embarrassed or demonstrates their feelings are hurt.

2. *There is always an "imbalance of power",* where one child is not comfortable reciprocating the teasing dialogue, or is not allowed to reciprocate.

At the end of the day, defining bullying is simple: *If one child asks another child to stop a specific behavior, or if the first child demonstrates he is upset and the teasing child does not stop, the second time the behavior occurs, it becomes bullying. Period. Simple.*

As you may have gathered, the definition is simple; however, reporting, addressing, and preventing bullying, as well as reforming behavior, are all significantly harder tasks. Yet, all of these are possible! It takes time, desire and patience. In the coming chapters we will address all of these challenges. There are examples across the nation, where school districts and communities have said, "enough", and have now contained the problem suc-cessfully. But first, let's look at how the bullying cycle works from a 50,000 view and then look at how many schools view bullying

LET'S BREAK IT DOWN: WHAT ARE THE COMPONENTS
AND SEQUENCE OF BULLYING?

Why is it important to understand the components of the bullying sequence and why is it important to know how a school typically views anti-bullying? The answer is, when your child is bullied, it is important to understand how a typical bullying cycle plays out in school and then how the school can help. First, we'll talk about how the bully cycle plays out.

THE INDIVIDUAL BULLYING CYCLE

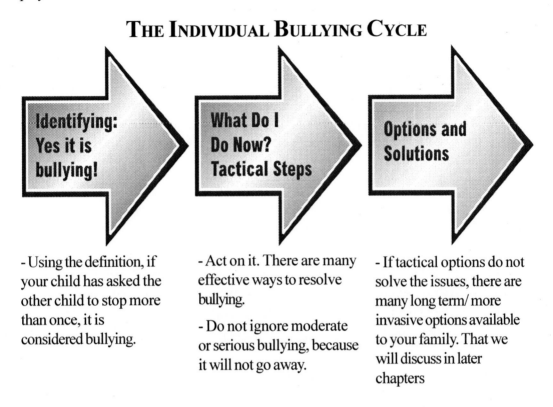

Identifying: Yes it is bullying!

- Using the definition, if your child has asked the other child to stop more than once, it is considered bullying.

What Do I Do Now? Tactical Steps

- Act on it. There are many effective ways to resolve bullying.

- Do not ignore moderate or serious bullying, because it will not go away.

Options and Solutions

- If tactical options do not solve the issues, there are many long term/ more invasive options available to your family. That we will discuss in later chapters

Sometimes the first part of the cycle, where a family is determining if it is bullying, is the most disconcerting. There is a great deal of uncertainty, and this is the point at which some tend to just "hope and wish it away." While once in a very great while it does go away, sadly, it seldom happens. Our refrain is, and always will be, "Ignoring it will not make it go away and often makes it worse." Addressing it early, and comprehensively, will make it go away.

In the following chapters, we will discuss identifying bullying, tactical steps to address it, and long-term options and solutions to get beyond the torment. Before we do that, let's take a look at a typical school program and the common weaknesses in the anti-bullying program.

THE TYPICAL SCHOOL ANTI-BULLYING PROGRAM SEQUENCE

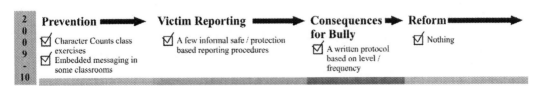

2009-10	**Prevention** ➡	**Victim Reporting** ➡	**Consequences for Bully** ➡	**Reform** ➡
	☑ Character Counts class exercises ☑ Embedded messaging in some classrooms	☑ A few informal safe / protection based reporting procedures	☑ A written protocol based on level / frequency	☑ Nothing

While many schools have this type of weak program, others have much more robust and effective programs. The above program is the typical version in most U.S. schools today. Sadly, some have considerably less than this program.

The following are the most common challenges schools are experiencing with anti-bullying programs, and are the reasons most often cited for not developing a strong and effective anti-bullying and bullying consequence protocol.

- Funding a large scale pre-packaged *prevention program* that is steeped in teaching team-building, acceptance, tolerance, awareness, and problem solving is expensive and some parents will object based on the fact it takes time away from general academics.

→ To which, we say, with all due respect, "Ridiculous!" If children do not feel safe and comfortable in their surroundings, no amount of academic program spending will increase their learning capacity or scores. Teaching them how to work together is time well spent and pays great dividends as they get older.

- Equally challenging is developing a bullying *reporting system,* or tool, for both victims and bystanders. Both victims and bystanders fear retaliation. In turn, schools fear three things:

    1. School leaders think children will not feel safe in reporting, and they believe there is nothing they can do to make children feel safer doing so. In the end, most school leaders give up and do not offer reporting systems.

    2. School leaders think they will receive an unmanageable amount of reports, and they will not be able to address them all effectively.

    3. School leaders will get complaints from parents about unfair treatment of their children if their children are reported as bullies.

→ To which, we say, with all due respect, "We understand, but, stand up, protect your kids and work hard to ensure the safety of your students and do it now." The key here is common sense. Yes, reports of bullying need to be vetted and investigated to determine validity in each case. If you vigorously encourage and incent children in a positive way, they will begin to report and to learn which behaviors are bullying and which are not. If you make it safe to report by developing anonymous reporting tools that are accessible, children will report more readily. If you change children's attitudes, school culture, and make it "uncool" to be a bully, children will report bullying freely. The key is actively investigating all reports, and in turn, children will believe it is beneficial to report the bullying.

- *Consequence protocols* designed to clearly document a standardized punishment system for all bullies is very difficult to create effectively. On one end of the spectrum, some will feel it is too harsh, and on the other end, some will feel it is weak and ineffective. Others will claim there is no way to define what is best, except on a case-by-case scenario.

  → To which, we say, "Yes, it will be difficult to develop a protocol, but if a team of folks with many perspectives come together and agree on a framework, schools *can* achieve this goal." It requires time and effort, but is well worth it. Most experts will agree an appropriate consequence, not necessarily a punishment, can be a teachable moment and an attitude changer for life. *Consequences for bullies have proven to be one of the main ingredients in re-teaching empathy, which facilitates introspection, and ultimately change, as well as learning how to accept others. When this happens, bullying is no longer an option.*

- *Reforming a bully is tricky.* The key here is to create introspection and ultimately, empathy toward his victims. School leaders will complain that, again, this can be a time consuming and expensive program to develop.

  → To which, we say, "Absolute nonsense!" These programs can be home grown and implemented by social workers, teacher and/or parents. Reforming bullies is critical. Right now, it is documented that nearly 60% of bullies will be prosecuted in our legal system by 24 years of age. This number can be reduced significantly if we reshape attitudes and beliefs before 14 years of age.

All of these school obstacles tend to get in the way of truly solving the problem. Knowledge is power, however, and it is important for families to understand the resources available to use at their school and the obstacles to avoid. Understanding your current school policy and anti-bullying program is critical in using the information to your advantage to solve the problem. We will discuss how to leverage this knowledge in later chapters.

Since knowledge is power, and understanding your audience helps you speak more effectively, let's discuss the bully.

WHAT TYPES OF KIDS ARE BULLIES?

There are four primary types of bullies.

The longer answer is based on a wide variety of experts' opinions and personal experiences. All of them are capable of bullying in a variety of ways that include, but are not limited to, person-to-person, electronic, cyber or other forms of bullying contact.

1. The Experimenter: This bully is merely "trying it on for size", on one or more occasions, and is generally between the ages of eight and fourteen years old. For the most part, this child learns empathy or discerns right from wrong over time. Most importantly, the child typically stops the first time he sees truly hurt feelings. These children are able to be reformed and sometimes grow to be protectors and defenders of victims. Characteristics include:

a. Experimentation with ways to gain social status

b. Desperately trying to figure out social status

c. Comes from any socioeconomic status

d. May have self-esteem issues

e. Likes attention

f. For the most part, a stable and well-behaved child, but just seeking power temporarily

2. The Old-Fashioned Bully: Typically, this child bullies others to fit in. He found out early in life that by making others look inadequate in some way, he will get a laugh, attention, or may gain respect from others out of fear of being bullied. Characteristics include:

a. Very low self-esteem

b. Starved for attention

c. Compulsive

d. Lack of self-control with very little self-awareness

e. Is probably being bullied by an adult

f. Does not have adequate parental guidance, love, and support

g. Is a highly-practiced liar, sometimes pathologically

3. The Elite Bully: Most often, this child is genuinely self-confident and gets a strange thrill or buzz from bullying. Paradoxically, this type of bully can be a very good student, or an elite athlete, and is very popular at school and well thought of by adults. Characteristics include:

a. Told for entire life that he is very special and "better" than others

b. Has been over-indulged

c. Acts out, lacks control, and desperately wants control

d. Acts like a leader and is well-behaved in front of adults

e. Feels entitled and invincible

f. Highly impulsive and is frequently obsessive

g. Is an excellent liar and gets a thrill from getting away with both lying and bullying

h. Actually enjoys being cruel and feels good about it

i. Excellent actors and salespeople

4. The Former Victim Turned Bully: Perhaps the most fragile emotionally, these children are quite angry. Some experts say these children have the highest risk for self-harm or for harming others. These children have concluded that the only way to escape being bullied is to bully others. Characteristics include:

a. Feeling guilty

b. Constantly rationalizing

c. Low self-esteem

d. Anxious

e. Uncomfortable alone

f. Have inadequate love and support

g. Feeling betrayed

h. Starved for positive reinforcement regarding self-worth

WHAT ARE THE VARIOUS TYPES OF BULLYING?

While bullying can be implemented in many ways, subtly and overtly, as well as in-person, through social media, online or through electronics, cell phones/phones, bullying can also mutate from one form to another. In most cases, it starts out with one bully, but can frequently mutate into other forms:

- **Lone Bullying:** One-on-one (popular/aggressive child vs. milder child)

- **Gang Bullying:** A team of popular children, the aggressors, tries to humiliate one less popular child, or children. Often, each member of this gang will choose a role and tactic to spread out over time to torment their victims.

- **Strategic Network Bullying:** When one bully, or a gang of bullies, actually puts a plan together to torment one or more children in-person, through electronics, and/or online. Frequently, this will accompany malicious rumor spreading, such as "I hate Jo clubs" and other viral tactics. These strategies are designed to *freeze out* the victim, so his social status is ruined partially, or completely. The plan is executed clearly and deliberately over time.

- **Aggressive Exclusion:** Where one bully, or a gang of bullies, has lobbied an entire class to exclude and ignore a child or group of children. This can happen in tandem with any of the above.

As you can see, the topic itself is complicated and important to understand. Just as important to understand, bullying can be addressed and resolved, even in quite severe cases. We have done it and you can too.

In fact, the next chapter will help guide you through *getting to the bottom of it* when you suspect your child is being bullied. We will take you through the first steps toward a solution, which is identifying bullying and understanding who, what, why and where. From there, we will provide you with a systematic guide to handling the situation and finding successful solutions.

LESSONS LEARNED

- Understanding the epidemic proportions of this issue will help you under stand why it gets ignored and why it goes continually unchecked in schools and communities.

- Bullying is easy to define; don't let people who are not interested in solving the issue tell you it is "hard to define." If you are trying to stop your child from being bullied, do not let others claim it is not bullying, if you feel it is. *This is less about specific definitions and more about how another child's behaviors are affecting and hurting your child.*

- It is useful to understand what type of bully is tormenting your child and the type of bullying behavior it is before you begin to solve the issue.

- Understand your school's program and push the school to use all of the program resources available to help solve your child's situation.

CHAPTER THREE
GETTING TO THE BOTTOM OF IT

Children Have Told Us:

- "I didn't tell my parents for two months. I didn't know how to tell them."

- "I knew my dad would go crazy if I told him what was happening to me, so I did not tell him."

- "I just kind of hinted to my mom that something was going on at school. I told her it was happening to a friend."

- "It's so humiliating I can't talk about it."

- "I was too embarrassed to tell anybody. I told my friend what happened and later I told her I was not telling the truth. I was afraid my friends would call me a tattler."

Parents Have Told Us:

- "My child got in the car after school and was crying. He told me that it was going on for five weeks."

- "I was tucking my daughter into bed one night and she started telling me she was sad about something her friends were doing. I just let her talk and she told me everything."

- "It was not easy to get my daughter to tell me what happened. It would come in bits and I had to piece it all together."

SIGNALS YOUR CHILD IS BEING BULLIED

It is not always easy to tell if your child is being bullied or just going through normal growing up moodiness. My child (J.E. DiMarco) was always very consistent with his moods–never really sad or in a bad mood. During the first few weeks of the bullying incidents, I noticed some very different behaviors. He did not want to go to school; he was always feeling sick and did not want to leave the house. I also noticed he was having nightmares and whimpering quite a bit in his sleep–something that had rarely happened to him in the past. Other parents have reported noticing a wide variety of other changes in behavior, such as eating or sleeping too much or too little.

Behavior Changes Parents Have Noticed in Their Children

- Acting differently in general
- Frequent sicknesses such as stomach aches and headaches
- Looking down frequently
- Avoiding eye contact
- More somber moods
- School work suffering
- Eating more or less than usual
- Difficulty sleeping, or sleeping more hours
- Agitated and jumpy
- Paranoid
- Asking what if questions, such as "What if I were home schooled?"
- Spending many hours reading or studying–even when other kids are around and being social
- Quieter in class, lunch, and recess
- Skipping school and social events
- Increased isolation in his room, or alone more frequently
- Not wanting to participate in any sports or activities outside of school
- Crying, moody, depressed, angry
- Increased fighting with siblings and parents
- Nightmares

These are just some of the many signs your child might be exhibiting if he is being bullied. The important thing to look for is a difference in typical behavior. Many signs could be easily ignored and explained away by hormonal changes or typical childhood phases. As a parent, it is time to do some detective work and get down to the bottom of these behavioral changes.

Getting to the bottom of the situation sometimes is no easy task for parents. Some kids will come right out and tell you everything, and others might take a little bit more investigating. Opening the lines of communication between you and your child during this very stressful time in a family's life can actually be an unexpected silver lining in this entire unfortunate situation. Although we can do without the stress of bullying, the love and support you show your child now will make the difference for the rest of his life.

WHO, WHAT, WHERE, WHY AND WHEN?

If you suspect your child is being bullied at school, you will need to get the facts. It is important to act quickly so that you can help your child resolve the situation as soon as possible and to prevent any long-term repercussions. Sometimes you have an hour or more to plan for a conversation with your child, but often you need to fly by the seat of your pants and hope for the best. If you have time to plan, or can plan a follow-up conversation with your child, getting to the facts is a bit easier if you know what you need to accomplish. You need to know *who* is involved, *what* happened, and *where* it happened. And, of course, *why* it took place, and then, *when* to help.

FORMAL VS. INFORMAL CONVERSATIONS

I often open up many conversations with my children with the reminder that they can always come to their dad and me at any time of day and any place no matter how bad a situation may seem to be. We are always there for them. A formal, sit-down family meeting works for many families, as well. Sometimes, it is just necessary to sit down and discuss things openly. Some parents have told me it is the only way to get their children to focus on a particular situation and to get the facts. They do not necessarily set a time to talk; they just let it happen when the time is right and other children, television, and texts will not disturb them.

However, a formal sit down is not my favorite choice. It often makes me feel uncomfortable, as this was the method my mother chose for me. I always knew when I was in trouble, or something bad had happened, when my mom said, "Sit down. We need to talk." She still tries to do this with me today, and I remind her how much I dislike sitting down to do anything.

Informality is best for our family. I found the easiest way to get my child to talk is to do a physical activity with him that he thoroughly enjoys. Since he likes the outdoors, I find it best to walk the dog, go fishing, take a hike or bike ride. On the flip side, he really enjoys video games so I have often played Wii games with him to initiate conversations during those activities. Let me tell you, even though I stink at Guitar Hero, he appreciates my effort, and thinks it is fun to have his parents battle it out for a spot in his band.

I always have the conversations without my younger son in the room or anywhere within earshot–that kid can hear everything, even when no one is speaking directly to him. Plus, he always adds his two cents and often makes the situation worse. "If I were you, I would just…" He then tells someone else–my mom, my sisters, his friends. This just makes a complicated situation even more complex. His older brother feels betrayed, yet again, and isolates himself even more.

I make every effort to have my husband part of the conversation. We want our son to know he is supported by both of his parents. My husband helps me document the facts. I often feel overwhelmed with emotion, causing me to miss some of the details. We often rehash what our child said to make sure we both understood what happened exactly the same way.

Our son does not always like Dad being involved in the initial conversation or activity. He feels embarrassed and prefers to talk to my husband after I give him the details. I think this happens because my son feels he can be completely open and emotional with me, if needed, and does not like his dad to see him being less than a man.

BE PATIENT, SKIP THE INTERROGATION

My career outside of being a mother is a human resource consultant. I have spent the past twenty years asking candidates behavior-based questions to determine if they are qualified for a position. I am paid to dig for details by asking open-ended questions and probing for specifics. This works well in my career, but often backfires as a parent. When talking with my son, I easily become frustrated with the pace of details I receive. One of the biggest mistakes I have made, time and time again in the past few years, is that I fire question after question at my child. Hammering my son with questions was the perfect way for him to completely shut me off.

It is best to be patient and let a child dictate the amount and pace of details. One or two open-ended questions seem to work best. After asking one question and your child begins to answer, do not ask another question, even if there seems to be an unnatural pause in the conversation. Your body language can show that you are very much engaged–a touch on the shoulder, a hug, or eye contact. Ask your child a follow-up question, as necessary, to get him to continue to talk openly about the situation.

Examples of Some Good Questions

- Can you tell me what happened?
- How did it start? How did it end?
- Who else was there?
- Were there any adults nearby?
- What did the bystanders say or do?
- What was said?
- Were you physically touched or harmed?

- How did this make you feel?

- What did you say or do?

- Did you tell anyone this happened?

- How long ago did it start?

- Who else is involved?

Obviously, you don't have to ask every single one of these questions, but use the questions as a guide to initiate a conversation. It sometimes takes several conversations to get all of the details.

DOCUMENT EVERYTHING!

Document all of the details of any bullying situation, even if it is for only your own records. Explain to your child why you are documenting this information. It might be needed in the future to bring the situation to the attention of the school or other authorities. After you document the child's circumstances, review the documentation with the child to make sure that all the facts are correct, including everyone involved. Sometimes I find after a couple of hours have gone by and things have settled down a bit, more details will surface. Also, make sure your child is not embellishing the facts, and is providing accurate details. You don't want to falsely accuse any other family.

You might want to reach out to parents of children (bystanders) who were involved to see if they would talk to their child about it, or to see if their child said anything to them about the situation. If you know the bystander child well, you might want to talk to them personally. Follow the same line of questioning–open ended, non-threatening. I called the parent of a bystander and asked if it was okay to talk to their son. I did get significantly more details from the bystander child and found out that the situation was much more serious than my son had told me. I ended the conversation asking the child not to discuss our talk with any other friends to avoid inadvertently making things worse.

We will discuss taking action in the next chapter. One thing we have learned is that the longer you wait, the worse the situation will get. The longer your child does not fight back, even if fighting back means getting a parent or teacher involved, the longer the humiliation will continue, often getting worse or escalating. The longer your child is isolated by this situation, the longer it will take him to get back to his old self and feel healthy again.

WHY ME?

Your child might have a few questions for you. One of the questions parents are often asked by their child is, "Why me?" There may, or may not, be a reason why the bully targets your child. Bullies tend to pick on children who typically do not defend themselves. Quiet, unassuming children seem to be a good target because they *look* like they

25

will not fight back. However, and this is an important *however*, all types of children are targeted. They can be average to very smart, standard attractiveness to very beautiful, or thin to overweight. Frequently, it is simply random selection. Bullies do not always have a criteria; it is merely impulsive.

Your child needs to be reassured that there is nothing wrong with him. The bully is the one with many problems, and unfortunately, he is taking it out on your child. Let your child know that together you will solve this problem and stop the bullying.

SOME FACTS ABOUT BULLIES TO SHARE WITH YOUR CHILD

Many children feel that their parents just will not understand. Explain to your child that this unattractive behavior has been around for years. It happened when you were in school. It happened when grandma was in school, and it happened when great grandma was in school. If you were ever bullied, or know someone who was, let your child know. This demonstrates you can relate to this issue.

If your kids are anything like ours, being mean to another is just not an option in their lives. As parents, we just would not allow it and correct it each and every time we witness it. I do not think it would ever cross my son's mind to be nasty to someone other than his brother–even as spiteful as he may be to his brother at times, it is minimal compared to the bullying he received from a stranger. Without getting too deep into the psychology of a bully, it is important that your child understands that bullying is not a normal or acceptable behavior. *This is worth repeating, bullying behavior is not normal behavior and should not be accepted by anyone for any reason.*

Explain to your child why bullies sometimes bully. Perhaps they are looking for attention. They might be bullied by others and are acting out. They might see bullying in their own home. Frequently, they are trying to be popular or funny. Oddly, by putting somebody else down, it makes them feel better about themselves. There are endless reasons why a bully may bully, but make it clear that your child understands the problem is not his fault. The problem is with the bully.

The bully will continue to bully unless he is stopped. Bullying is an imbalance of power and he wants your child to feel powerless or helpless. Ignoring the situation often fuels the fire of the bully. The more isolated the victim, the more powerful the bully feels.

But the good news is that the bully can be stopped. In some cases, once bullies realize that the victim is strong enough to stand up to them by telling them to knock it off, or by telling a trusted adult, they often move on to someone else or hopefully stop all together.

WHERE TO GO FOR HELP AT SCHOOL?

Should another situation arise, your child needs some ideas of where to go for help. Discuss with your child who he trusts at school–a teacher, principal, nurse, and social worker, even the school secretary. Pick a person or two that your child could go to, and make them aware, with just a few details, of what is happening so they keep an extra eye out if your child is looking for help.

FOLLOW-UP QUESTIONING

After the initial onset of bullying, it is so important to keep the conversations ongoing. Hopefully, it does not have to be part of a conversation every day, but by keeping the lines of communication open with your child you will be aware of any incident no matter how small. When your child gets home from school or from a social event, watch his behavior, facial expressions, and mood. You can follow up with some more open-ended questions.

Some Questions You Might Consider Asking

- Who did you eat lunch with today? What did you talk about?
- Did you do anything special at recess?
- How was your walk home? Did you see anybody interesting?
- How was your bus ride home? Is there anybody on the bus you don't particularly care for? Why not?
- Do you want to have friends over this weekend? Anybody new?

Depending on the answer, you can pretty much figure out if your child is still being bullied. Remember, often after a bully is reprimanded, he stops for a few months and might even go out of his way to be exceptionally, but insincerely, nice to your child. He may or may not start up again. Be watchful for reoccurrences. Some bullies are so bold that they find any opportunity to start up again, but on the second round of bullying, they become cleverer and have developed a covert way of operating. They bully when adults are not watching. Then they try a different bullying tactic such as recruiting others to bully the child or spreading rumors across a grade level.

KEEP IT WITHIN YOUR FAMILY

Being bullied is such an isolating time, and I hate to suggest that your family isolate themselves even more, but it is important that you are mindful of who you discuss the situation with outside of your family. Be careful whom you tell in your community. I suggest keeping it to your close friends and family. Sometimes when acquaintances ask you questions about it, they inadvertently make things worse for your child and your family by discussing it with other members of the community and their children. It becomes like the game of telephone where incorrect details are often added to this story and may just thrill the bully when they find out. Sometimes other mothers like to stir the pot by having the latest and greatest thing to discuss at the grocery store, tennis or a PTA meeting. Protect your child by keeping details to a minimum and only sharing information with a few trusted folks.

COMFORTING YOUR CHILD

One of the worst statements you can share with your child is the *need to toughen up*. Yes, it is important for your child to first try to take care of the situation by being assertive, confident and saying stop. If this is not working, or if you have a child that is non-confrontational, all the toughening up in the world is not going to work. It is just not in a child's genetic makeup. Being non-judgmental will increase your child's trust in you. Make certain your child knows that you will not act without consulting him first.

Your child needs to be comforted and supported and to feel loved during this very difficult time for all of you. Praise your child for talking to you and reassure him that you will not do anything to embarrass him. Do things as a family, so that your child feels less isolated. The theme in our home is that we are in this together and together we can stop this behavior.

MANAGING *YOU*

It is very challenging to keep your emotions in check as a parent when discussing the bullying of your child. As I learned about the details of my son's bullying, I wanted to scream and cry, and then I wanted immediately to call the school and the child's parents before I had all the details.

It is so difficult on the parents, as well as the child, and parents do need to let their stress out, but it needs to be done behind closed doors. It is important for you to let your emotions out so go ahead, scream and cry. Just do it when your child is not around. Your child does not want to upset you or humiliate you in any way. It is important that your child continues to trust you. One of the best ways to do that is by not over reacting during the discussions. I found it best to take pauses and deep breaths before I asked my next question.

Most importantly, keep calm as much as you can, and demonstrate to your child that he is protected, and loved, and that you are addressing the situation with vigor. This instills confidence and hope.

LESSONS LEARNED

- If you have time, plan your questions in advance when you are trying *to get to the bottom of it*. Be patient as you are asking your child questions.

- Try not to make your child feel quizzed, and do more listening than talking.

- Reassure the child that he did nothing wrong, and that he has nothing to be ashamed of because the bully is the one with the problem.

- Document all facts.

- Keep the details of the situation within your own family, so that it does not become the talk of the town.

- Try to keep life as normal as possible.

- Take care of yourself too.

Chapter Four
Once You Know Your Child Is Being Bullied, What Are The Next Steps?

"It has been going on so long, and has gotten so deeply embedded at school, we don't know where to begin!"

"Our daughter tried to make it stop, but could not make it happen. This child is nasty to the core to my child. We had suspected something was going on, but not like this. We knew about some light teasing, but never guessed it would grow into this mess."

Many Solutions. Few Are Easy, But They Do Work

Bullying is tough to manage due to the wide variety of ways the bully implements the offenses. Bullying can be infrequent and light in nature, or vicious and constant. Every case is unique. What is not unique is the clear need to stop the torment for your child. Children bully for ridiculous and cruel reasons, and some bully for no reason at all. The important message: STOP IT EARLY. DO NOT LET IT GO ON. STOP IT COMPREHENSIVELY. MAKE SURE YOU CONFRONT EVERY SINGLE BULLY. If you let bullying persist, it will only get worse and will spread to other bullies.

There are many solutions to bullying, and every solution will be different based on a child's unique circumstances. Once a parent identifies the bullying incidence, there are steps that can effectively manage the situation to achieve a positive solution.

1. First, stay calm. This is the hardest thing to do, but is the most important. When you talk to the school, or another parent, you want to appear as the engaged, caring parent, not the *crazy parent*.

2. Document everything. Every time your child comes home with a story, write down who, what, when, where and how.

3. Encourage your child to talk freely, and remind him there is no judgment at home. Ask specifically about how it makes him feel and if there is anything that can make it better. Let him know right away that the bullying situation will be addressed, and he will be protected.

4. DO NOT IGNORE IT. DO NOT TELL YOUR CHILD TO IGNORE IT. It is now officially bullying. Occasionally, with the bully who is an experimenter, ignoring it may work, but with advanced bullies, ignoring it is useless. While ignoring it once is a good first step, do not do so after the first event. Most advanced bullies feel powerful when their victims ignore it.

5. Sometimes, smaller, subtle techniques work with bullies, sometimes not, Try to develop a few tactics with your child to address the bully. These tactics will only work if the bullying is in the first few weeks; otherwise, they generally are not successful. However, if your child can execute them early, it may be the medicine needed for his bully.

   a. Use humor to diffuse the situation. Example, "Yes, I am a geek, and proud of it just like Bill Gates and Steve Jobs were when they were my age."

   b. Tease the bully back. Not all children do this well or are comfortable with this, so role-play first if you think this it is viable—it may not be suited for your child's personality.

   c. Let the bully know the situation will not be tolerated with comments such as, "Not cool Dude, stop it." or "Maybe you don't understand that what you are doing is bothering me, but it really is, please stop." These comments only typically work with experimenting bullies, but could work with others.

   d. Take the bully off to the side, away from the limelight, and simply ask him to stop.

   e. Have your child partner with a more popular friend and ask the friend to make it clear to the bully that he is being rude and nasty, and the bullying needs to stop.

6. If the bullying includes social media, shut down all social media accounts immediately. See Chapter 15; it is devoted to this topic. Get a new cell phone number and private email account for your child. Before you shut down the account, consider sending a message to all of your child's tormenters indicating that if they do not stop now, and stop talking about your child in any way, you will go to all of the parents and the school to address it directly. Very important: KEEP A CLOSE EYE ON YOUR CHILD'S PHONE HISTORY. Review all texts, emails, social media exchanges, everything. This is critical. Minimize whom your child inter-

acts with electronically, and ensure there is no online or electronic bullying. Do not worry about being over-protective. It may be that you choose to stop the complete oversight after the bullying stops. For now, be vigilant and review everything. Make certain there is oversight of your child's computer usage to ascertain that he is not spending time on *dark solutions* sites or sites that give your child negative or harmful ideas.

7. Do not let anyone tell you it is just *kids being kids*. Let your child know that bullying is not acceptable, and he should not accept it. Bullying is abnormal behavior.

8. Do not allow your school to perform *peer-to-peer conflict resolution* where the victim and the bully meet in the same room to discuss the situation and problem-solve. This re-victimizes the victim. The bully learns nothing and simply says what the adult wants to hear so he can get back to being a bully as quickly as possible. The bully will be laughing about the meeting within minutes. The consensus is that conflict resolution does not work, and it actually makes the situation worse.

9. Do not blame your child for the bullying. Bullying is abnormal behavior, and a victim never deserves it or provokes it.

10. Make certain you work with your child and ask him how he wants to respond to the bullying and how he would like to handle the situation. Retaliation from the bully is a possibility, and you need to include that variable into your plan. Discuss a few options with your child to help address this issue.

11. If you disagree with the way your child manages the bullying, do not judge him. Make additional suggestions for him to try.

12. Praise your child for being brave and reporting the bullying–do this frequently.

13. Help your child see how reporting the bullying and addressing the situation is the only way to make it stop. Unfortunately, there will be some inevitable retaliation, and you will have to coach your child through that as well.

14. In serious, ongoing cases (three or more instances), call the school to map out a specifically tailored strategy for your child. Equally important, DO NOT LET THE SCHOOL IMPLEMENT ACTION UNTIL YOU HAVE REVIEWED THE PLAN WITH YOUR CHILD, AND DISCUSSED THE OPTION WITH THE SPECIFIC SCHOOL STAFF MEMBERS WHO WILL BE INVOLVED. YOU NEED TO BE COMFORTABLE WITH THE PLAN.

15. Key requirements for the plan should include:

   a. You, as the parent of the victim, must take an active role in the solution.

   b. The bully's parents must be called and notified.

   c. The bully must have a consequence or punishment.

   d. The bully and his family must sign an agreement to cease and desist all bullying, and to stop any further discussion regarding your child in any manner, to anybody, at any time. There are samples of this agreement in Chapter 17.

   e. The bully must be notified that many acts of bullying are considered crimes after a second offense. Let the bully know how your state's antibullying law will affect him should the bullying continue.

   f. The plan must have a specific timeline that the school is accountable for while correcting the problem.

   g. Your child needs to have *go-to* adults at school to help him.

16. Do not take, "I'm sorry there is nothing we can do", as an answer from either the bully's parent or the school.

17. Do not let the bullying go on too long; acting early and comprehensively will prevent the bullying from going viral throughout the school. If it not stopped early, it could go viral simply by other children copying the behavior, or if the bully is strategic, recruiting others to do the bullying after he has been reported and can no longer be seen bullying.

18. If the bullying is happening in a specific class or location, have a meeting with the teacher in charge of that location, and together develop a plan that the teacher will commit to implementing every day.

19. If your child is bullied with any regularity, the bully's parents must be told. Let the school handle it first. If they do not call the parents, or if the bullying has not stopped, *you* need to call the parents. Read Chapter 5 so you are prepared.

20. Make sure your child has a point person to sit with in each class, and develops new friendships and interests to protect his ego during this period. If your child has lost friends, try to help him make new ones and find new activities

21. Ask your child if he knows of an older child that is kind, well thought of, and popular in school. Seek out that family and find out if that child will watch out for your son or daughter, and intervene if your child is bullied at school or other places.

22. Make certain your child has protection at school to the best of your ability. Work with the school to have adults supervising open areas such as hallways, locker rooms, gym class, the bus, and other open, vulnerable situations.

23. Get a mentor for your child. Find an older child who remembers what it is like to be in the same grade as your child and will act as your child's guide through this time.

24. If your child has close friends, get them involved to help protect your child.

25. Help your child find new friends through clubs, groups, and throughout the community. These can be community centers, YMCA-based groups, park district classes or sports, library programs, collecting clubs, drama clubs, club sports, church groups, volunteer groups, and others. Get creative, and find your child a group who will embrace him.

26. Make certain you keep the lines of communication open so you are aware of new bullying that may occur.

27. Be a pleasant nuisance. Stay in touch initially with your child's teachers, school counselor, psychologist, and principal daily and weekly. Then retreat as needed as the problem subsides.

28. Consider a therapist for your child who is familiar with bullying trauma.

29. Importantly, if you are not getting the support you need at school, or in the community, visit your police department. Make it clear that initial steps have not worked, and you would like an officer to have a conversation with the bully and his parents.

From experience, it is a good idea to develop a checklist of all the steps to be taken to stop the bullying. And, be certain you are a role model and stay calm. Stay determined and focused. Be your child's advocate. Do not give up. If the steps outlined in this chapter do not work, there are additional, more invasive options discussed in Chapter Five that can be implemented. The set of steps and options in Chapter Five are more dramatic, but very effective.

LESSONS LEARNED

- Do not let bullying go on for very long. The longer it goes on, the more powerful the bully becomes.

- If you are comprehensive in the approach to stopping the bullying, there will be less retaliation, but there will always be exclusion after you stop the acts of bullying. Prepare your child for this and help him be strong. Remember that being ignored is better for self-esteem than being attacked every day. Regardless, your child will need extra love and support during this time.

- Put a plan in place and stay focused. Do not skip steps. Do not let anyone bully you into thinking you are over-reacting.

- Do not take "no" or "we can't do a whole lot about it" or "its just kids being kids" as an answer from school or the bully's parents. They *can* help to stop it, and it is not just "kids being kids."

- Stay calm, pleasant, but very direct with everyone.

CHAPTER FIVE
WHAT ADDITIONAL OPTIONS
ARE AVAILABLE TO SOLVE
THE PROBLEM?

"Nothing is working. My child is crying everyday, and I feel helpless. I just want to scream!"

I remember talking to friends who had taken all of the recommended steps in Chapter Four, but the bullying continued. They said that because the bullies had not received a real consequence from the school or the parents, the bullying became worse. The bullies were retaliating. This does happen, and yes, it is important to implement consequences even after the first incident. While the steps in Chapter Four can work, there may be need for additional options and solutions.

There are some key things to remember about families with bully children.

1. Parents of bullies need specifics and have a hard time believing it is happening, so documenting all incidents as much as possible is critical to taking the next set of steps.

2. A wide variety of parents exists. Some parents of bullies would like to be notified about unacceptable behavior displayed by their children. Others will deny the behavior because of embarrassment, shame, or arrogance. Others simply do not care and do not want to be bothered.

3. Most parents of bullies do have, at the very least, *some inkling* their child is bullying, but clearly have not addressed this behavior with their child.

4. When addressing parents, they may not know of the specific type of bullying imposed on your child, so, in fairness, keep this in mind as you approach them. Patiently recount and describe the bullying acts and provide specifics.

5. Be prepared that many parents of bullies will not apologize. You will find some great parents who are objective and will address their child's behavior with assertiveness and thoroughness. Many, however will ignore you, and never be accountable for their child's actions.

6. You have law enforcement options, with degrees of action, at your disposal. Partner with your police department. They are there to help you, and they are free. Sometimes, just a visit and conversation between the police officer and the bully child will stop the abhorrent behavior.

Keeping all of the above in mind, if the school has not been successful in stopping the bullying behavior, you need to take action. And, do it now. It will not get better. Remember, the longer you wait, the more entrenched the bullying behavior becomes, and the deeper your child's self-esteem plummets. Further, the bullying is likely to spread because other children will think they can get away with it with your child.

What are the next steps?

1. As uncomfortable as it is, it is important to start with a calm phone call to the parents of the bully. Prepare for this phone call and have specifics, such as dates and times. Think through your comments before you deliver them. The parents of the bully will want details.

2. Be open and objective, but do not be manipulated. Do not let the parents of the bully talk you into believing it is just "kids being kids." They may also indicate they had no idea. On the positive side, they may say, "I was not aware of it, but I will talk to my child and call you back." You should hope for that positive response, but be prepared to hear that they were not aware or indicate you must be wrong.

3. If this phone call does not result in stopping the bullying, your next step is to develop a written agreement between both families. The school or another neutral party can facilitate the discussion, or you can have the conversation directly with the family. The key components are:

   - Both children should agree not to talk to each other or at each other.

   - Both children should agree not to talk about the other child to others, not even in code or online.

   - Both children should agree that they will not discuss the solution or the agreement with anyone.

   - If other children approach the bully child and want to gossip or talk about the incidents related to the child that was bullied, the bully child is to respond by saying, "I don't know what you are talking about", and walk away.

- The bully child should understand he is not allowed to recruit others to bully the victim in any manner, shape, or form.

- Both families should sign the document and a copy should be kept at school and with each family.

If for any reason the aforementioned steps do not work or are not feasible, the next set of steps should be swift.

1. Have the bully's schedule changed so that your child does not need to see the bully in any of his classes. If this is not possible, get your child's schedule changed.

2. Have an informational meeting with a police officer at the station in your community and determine if you can press charges. Bring all of your documentation to this meeting. If you do not have documentation, bring your stories with specific details. Even at young ages, the state or federal harassment, verbal assault, assault and battery or slander laws may apply and you can press charges. If your child's harassment does not stop, at least ask a police officer to visit the home of the bully when a guardian is present and have the officer discuss the next steps if the bully does not stop.

3. It may be worthwhile to consult an attorney to determine if a written contract has more weight than the previously listed agreement. Or more aggressively, determine if there is the option for a civil suit against the school or family. We do not recommend this course of action at this stage. This should be the final resort.

4. Once you have done this research, and before you go further, you should contact the bully's parents by mail, email, or a phone call. Let them know that you are frustrated because the bullying is continuing, and that you are considering legal action and pressing charges. If they do not contact you, then and only then, should you go back to law enforcement and an attorney.

5. Either the police or the attorney may present other options, such as having the officer or attorney call or visit the bully parents and issue an order of protection.

6. Regardless, having a recorded visit on file at the police department is important as you decide the next steps.

Let's pause here and talk a little bit about the repercussions of the above actions. This likely will get the attention of the bully's parents, but will also make them angry. When parents in a community feel attacked, they attack back. In return, they may seek legal advice or law enforcement assistance. Realistically, they may have a bigger, more power-ful attorney. This is why it is important to document the schools' actions, the police visit, and the ensuing discussions with the officer, and keep a file at the police station and in your home prior to taking any criminal action. Equally important to understand, is the need to galvanize support around you with friends and family.

ADDITIONAL OPTIONS AND SOLUTIONS

You do have other options if the bullying continues. You can consider these options before you engage law enforcement or legal counsel as a viable alternative, or use these options if the previously mentioned actions do not work.

1. Talk to your school superintendent. By law, they must see you and must address your concerns. Be polite, firm and clear. Bring something in writing in terms of your requests.

2. Talk to the school board and make certain they are aware of the same requests.

3. Make everyone accountable and put it in writing.

Most school boards and school superintendents do not like bad publicity, so it is important to start out politely, but demand action. If they do not put together an effective plan quickly, you can then initiate more dramatic and significant actions.

MORE SIGNIFICANT SOLUTIONS

If none of the above has proven successful, a few significant, but invasive options are available:

1. Contact your police department and local government and get an order of protection. Officials will help you process the order and have it enforced. This will temporarily require that the bully have a restraining order.

2. If a family has resources, and it is the right thing for their child, transferring the child to a private school or other school in a neighboring town is effective and provides the victim with full relief. This is invasive, but does take the stress away. Frequently, bullied children like this option even though they know it will require making new friends and learning a new school system.

3. Alternately, most states have a "Safe Schools Law" which mandates that if a public school is found to be unsafe for a child for any reason, the school is required by law to find another public school for the child to attend. The new school should be within a reasonable distance from the current school, with transportation provided. Parents can transfer their child and tuition is not required.

4. Another option is moving to another town, county or state. This is the ultimate fresh start. In a few instances, when job and employment opportunities for the parents are available, this may make some sense.

5. Home schooling is popular now, and can be a last resort option. In many communities, the local YMCA or park district offers gym classes or social events for home-schooled children to supplement the home curriculum.

6. If you want to stay in the community and school, but no one will listen and help you, consider the media. Getting the attention of a newspaper or investigative reporter can help your cause. Investigative reporters love these types of stories.

As you can see, there are many options. They have been provided sequentially, but can be used in various chronologies depending on your own individual case.

The following is an abbreviated success story.

A child who had been bullied since fourth grade had tried many of the recommendations. The family finally decided to transfer schools in seventh grade. The child at first was quite upset, but within two months, he had found a new friend, and his self-esteem rebounded significantly.

From there, he went to private high school that his parents financed with a loan, where he made life-long friends who he has stayed close with through, and after, college. He recently graduated from a small Northeastern college with a master's degree, and was one of the first to secure a job in his field during a deep recession.

Sometimes the ending is not quite this happy, but most of the time, when you are not afraid to make a bold move, it reaps dividends for your child. Of course, there is much to consider including your other children, costs, stress, transportation, tuition, employment, and many other variables. That said, fresh starts are defined in a million different ways. A fresh start does not necessarily need to be a bold move; it can be something more subtle, but have the same effect.

We will continue to talk about solution-driven ideas, and other resources for families and communities. There are many more ideas. Keep reading.

LESSONS LEARNED

- Document everything.

- Gather counsel and ideas BEFORE EXECUTING; assimilate all of the advice.

- Be confident.

- Stay focused.

- Talk to your police department for ideas.

- Involve your superintendent and school board earlier rather than later if you are not getting the help you need.

- Do not be afraid of a bold move. Children adapt well over time.

- Consider a therapist for your child to prevent depression or further challenges to their self-esteem.

- Use all of your community resources:

  a.   School social workers

  b.   Superintendent

  c.   School Board

  d.   School nurse

  e.   Therapists

  f.   Psychologists

  g.   Coaches

  h.   Mentors

  i.   Older children

  j.   Park districts

  k.   Clinics

  l.   YMCAs and Boys & Girls Clubs

  m.   Sports teams/groups

CHAPTER SIX
WHAT ELSE CAN BE DONE?

The majority of the time bullying starts at school. Schools, by law, are responsible for providing a safe environment for our children to learn. The Civil Rights Act protects citizens, including children, youth and students, from discrimination based on class, gender, religion, race, age, national origin, sexual orientation, political party and disability. Most parents often do not consider bullying as a violation of their child's civil rights. We certainly did not. Parents and schools also do not view bullying as a crime punishable by law enforcement. Bullying **is a violation** of your child's civil rights. There are many community and municipal resources available for us, as parents, to use to help our children when bullied.

WHAT CAN WE DO AS PARENTS?

We have suggested that you contact the school first. If your school does not act swiftly and effectively, the next step involves doing additional homework in an effort to encourage your school to do more to resolve the situation.

We found that our schools did not have a strong anti-bullying policy. When our children were harassed, we had a *Character Counts* program, which encourages children to be kind to one another. This is a great program, however, it does not directly discuss bullying and the damage it can cause to other children. The school also did not have a program to educate parents on what to do if their child was bullied.

Our district parent handbook had one paragraph regarding bullying. It stated that if your child feels uncomfortable about a situation, he should let an adult know. It did state that bullying and harassment at school, or in any event related to school, would not be tolerated. It went on to state that the school would work with *your* family to address the situation confidentially and with sensitivity. It did not mention any consequences that a bully might receive if he indeed was harassing another child. It did not state the name of anyone to specifically contact. It did not state that anything would be done, except that the situation would be addressed.

Many laws and policies require schools to keep our children safe. The United States Education Department Office of Civil Rights has recently increased their attention on bullying. They have held several anti-bullying summits that we were invited to attend. It is clear that the Education Department is going to mandate aggressively that all schools have policies and procedures in place to safeguard against bullying. In 2011, it is expected there will be several new anti-bullying laws in effect. The majority of states currently have anti-bullying laws in place, and they are reviewing them to make them more vigorous. But, currently, there are not any Federal anti-bullying laws.

WORKING WITH GOVERNMENT OFFICIALS

Do your homework. Research and make yourself familiar with your state's laws as they pertain to bullying. This information can be found by checking your state's website or by contacting your local State Representative or State Senator. A website we found particularly helpful was http://www.bullypolice.org. This site organizes all of the United States anti-bullying laws in one place. In addition, contact your Congressman and Senator via telephone and email encouraging them to get involved with developing federal anti-bullying laws. They usually have an intern that will relay the information to the elected official. Do not think you are bothering them. We all pay taxes, and they work to represent us as well as our children.

Ask your school for their written anti-bullying policies. Also, ask the school for a copy of the written anti-bullying procedures that teachers, staff and administrators use when a case of bullying is identified. If your school does not have a written policy and procedure, request that one be designed and ask that it be done in a timely manner. Follow-up with the school to see if they made any progress. If, after providing these subtle hints to your principal and your situation is still not resolved, consider contacting your superintendent and school board. We contacted both to discuss our children's situation and the lack of a solid anti-bully policy. Both leaders were receptive and concerned about our children and the bullying problem in general. As a result, our bullying issues were addressed and some steps were taken to correct all the problems. One result of our meetings was that attention to bullying increased and an anti-bullying task force was created to develop new guidelines and implement some of our suggestions.

During the time when our children were bullied, problems with bullying in our school district continued to escalate, and our school was not resolving the situation, so we continued to contact people who might be of some assistance. We contacted a county board member who, coincidentally, had been bullied himself. He brainstormed with us to create a list of elected officials, government employees, and government agencies that might be able to help. Since he was also a practicing attorney, he explained how bullying is a violation of our children's civil rights, and our children have the right to live without fear and intimidation. He had recently been contacted by a citizen whose son was hearing impaired and was bullied in high school. He told the parent that the child's rights under the

Americans with Disabilities Act of 1990, as well as the Rehabilitation Act of 1973, states that it is illegal to harass a child with special needs because of their disability and thereby cause interference with learning.

He also suggested we might consider contacting law enforcement and an attorney. We were pleasantly surprised by his willingness to assist us. He even followed up and put us in contact with the County Superintendent of Schools who happened to be an advocate for anti-bullying legislation. The County Superintendent was receptive and welcoming of our comments, concerns, and suggestions. She was aware of the bullying problems we had in our county, state and nation. She was willing to do what was necessary for us to resolve our situation. She taught us about The No Child Left Behind Act of 2001. This complicated Act implemented many actions that schools must take to keep our children safe. One area of the Act specifically required that the schools' support programs prevent violence in and around schools. The County Superintendent appointed us to be the parent representatives for our county on the anti-bullying task force, and to be the voice of the victims' parents. This was an honor we embraced enthusiastically. This was yet another opportunity for us to help our children, but also to help other children.

WORKING WITH THE LOCAL POLICE DEPARTMENT

Our next call was to the local police department to discuss if criminal charges could be pressed against the bully if the situation did not resolve. When contacting your local police department, request to speak with an officer who is typically assigned to schools in the community. We spoke to the Drug Abuse Resistance Education (D.A.R.E) representative. We were surprised to learn that our town already had an anti-cyber bullying task force. This task force was available for schools to use as a resource to discuss this increasingly popular form of bullying. When discussing cyber bullying, the officer explained that the school does have a responsibility to act on this type of bullying, even if it happens outside of school grounds. The justification for the school to get involved is the fact that cyber bullying affects the victim at school and his studies. This makes it necessary for the school to get involved. We discussed the possibility of pressing charges against the parents of the bully. The officer explained the parents could be charged with a misdemeanor for not properly supervising the child's activities. In addition to criminal charges, there has been civil litigation with possible financial consequences for the bully's family.

As an example, in the state of Illinois and in other states, it is a crime to forward sexually explicit pictures. Among youth, "sexting" is a crime and the person forwarding the picture(s), and in some cases the persons sending and receiving the picture, could be charged with a crime. A minor, in some cases, can be charged as an adult and receive serious consequences including jail time, which includes the requirement to be registered as a sexual predator.

Other crimes your local law enforcement may be able to charge a bully with include, but are not limited to, assault, stalking, harassment, robbery, and threatening death. It may not be necessary to go to these lengths, but it is valuable information to have when talking with your school and the bully's parents if the situation continues.

Repeatedly we hear that bullying is a normal part of adolescent behavior. There is absolutely nothing normal about it. Bullying is abuse and is a violation of your child's rights. By doing your homework and acting quickly, you will be able to get the situation contained. There are many places where you can go for help.

LESSONS LEARNED

- Make some noise, professionally but persistently.
- Know your rights and the laws in your state.
- There are people out there who care and will help. Just ask.
- Contact elected officials and government agencies. They are a good resource and have ideas on how to rectify the situation.
- Talk to your countywide Superintendent of Schools.
- File a criminal complaint, if necessary, with your local law enforcement.

Chapter Seven
LGBT (Lesbian, Gay, Bisexual and Transgender) Children as Targets

Just when we think we may have made some progress culturally as a society, another horribly tragic tale of a Lesbian, Gay, Bisexual and Transgender (LGBT) child being tormented by their peers or, in the worst cases, a suicide, appears in the media or in your own community.

While the rise in bullying of LGBT children seems to be forefront in the media, the crisis continues. The crisis continues primarily because parents of bullied LGBT children frequently feel powerless in these situations. The behavior is commonly swept under the rug by schools, and communities ignore the problem. If schools and communities took a leadership role in this challenge, the solutions would come faster. Better yet, there would be less depression and fewer suicides in children.

Bullies of LGBT children are typically the most insecure of all bully types. Those who bully LGBT children need to understand their actions, reflect upon the actions, and receive a specific consequence. Consequences are more successful than just a general punishment. It is challenging enough to know you are LGBT as a child, but a child bullied during that discovery is nothing short of excruciating.

We have spent time with many parents of LGBT children over the last couple of years, and the following story represents a typical, yet incredibly challenging, situation for parents and our schools today.

Terry

When Terry was 14, his Dad had a new career opportunity and he decided to move the family from an urban, progressive location to a suburban, traditional community. Terry, an attractive, well-dressed young man with a great singing voice, felt he was different from most kids at his new high school. In fact, deep down, he knew it.

Terry had been thinking about coming out of the closet for some time, but he wanted to wait until he settled into his new school and made friends. Unfortunately, that plan did not work well. Almost immediately, the "gay" jokes started. The athletes, the smart kids, and almost everyone, hassled him. Terry laughed it off at first. Terry tried to act and dress differently so that he would blend into the new environment.

None of this worked. He finally told his parents. The bullies were vicious and unrelenting. Sometimes they were physical. Terry was pushed, poked, tripped, spat upon, and worse, beat up in the locker room. Terry was adamant that his parents stay out of it. He felt that addressing it would only make it worse.

The social media torment became so disgusting that he terminated his Facebook membership and created an entirely new email account. Terry endured several months more of this with virtually no friends to lean on. Terry began drinking, staying in his room, and lashing out at whomever was handy.

Terry's Dad understood he needed to do something; he could not let his son continue to be treated this way. Young LGBT children who are bullied become isolated and can spiral into an unhealthy emotional state quickly. If your LGBT child is bullied there is help available, and there are means to stopping the torment.

BULLYING AND LGBT CHILDREN

Bullying of LGBT children has escalated and has become increasingly dangerous in the last several years. The U.S. Education Department released results in 2009 of the GLSEN's (Gay, Lesbian and Straight Education Network) National School Climate Survey. The survey found that 85% of LGBT students report being harassed in school due to their sexual orientation or to a perceived sexual orientation. Of the group, 63.7% of LGBT students report being harassed because of masculine or feminine traits they exhibit in appearance or behavior. Only 18% of the children surveyed reported the bullying event. What makes this type of bullying dangerous is that LGBT children are three times more likely to attempt suicide than other young children.

WHY DOES A BULLY TARGET AN LGBT CHILD?

LGBT children are generally more shy or introverted than other children. Since they often struggle with being gay or lesbian, they may isolate themselves from others because of it. Bullies pick on a vulnerable child, as he is often easier to abuse. These LGBT children feel uncomfortable with their identity. They do not want to tell a parent or adult that others harass them. The child often feels he deserves it. No child deserves or invites bullying, ever. It is the bully's issue, not the victim's issue.

ADULTS THAT BULLY LGBT CHILDREN

It is not just youth that bully LGBT children. Adults often participate in bullying as well. Sometimes, even a parent of a LGBT child bullies. Examples of harsh statements by an adult bully are "Be a man", or "Act like a girl, not a boy". An adult bully may say these things because they feel that it is their role to press their beliefs on a child. Adults often bully LGBT children based on gender, perhaps because they do not look or dress like other children. When discussing LGBT children with seemingly reasonable adults, we were astonished to find that some adults would look the other way if a LGBT child were bullied. It happens more often than you can imagine. Double standards are dangerous–sadly, there are adults who feel it is okay for a LGBT child to be bullied, but not a straight child. Changing the attitude of an adult may be more difficult than changing the attitude of a bully.

In a recent case, astonishingly, the parents of a group of high school bullies allowed their children to go to school wearing t-shirts that had an anti-gay message stating "Straight Pride", as well as a bible verse that may be interpreted as a death threat to LGBT children. The shirts were worn during an anti-bully week encouraging acceptance of all people gay, lesbian and straight. The school did not punish the children wearing the shirts, but asked that they not wear them to school. These judgmental statements made by these teenagers had to stem from somewhere. Most likely, they originated in the home or church environment. While many bullies adopt their bullying behavior from their parents, there are times when they are highly influenced by other homophobic adults in their lives. This happens far too often.

METHODS OF BULLYING AND THE REASONS

Physical and verbal harassment, the old-school bullying techniques, are still a favorite among bullies when it comes to LGBT harassment. The same offensive and disrespectful comments used for decades such as "sissy", "queer", and "dyke"; are being passed down from generation to generation as a means of passing judgment on LGBT children.

Cyber-bullying of LGBT children has become an even easier method of choice for the coward bully to violate another child. A coward bully is someone that will not bully another in person, but is comfortable bullying behind a computer keyboard. Death threats are more common online now because some children believe they can bully anonymously via the Internet.

Heterosexual boys bully homosexual boys more often than their female counterparts do. Homophobia may be a contributing factor. They might fear that the LGBT child is sexually interested in them, or maybe the opposite. There is a better than average chance the heterosexual child has some homosexual thoughts or fears. These homosexual thoughts are a common part of growing up for both genders; however, a child may not understand that it is normal. It is normal if you are gay, straight or polka-dotted. Some children have a difficult time accepting the fact they are experiencing these thoughts. In turn, as a means to vanquish these thoughts, a child will demean the closest seemingly assumed gay, or established LGBT, child. The irony here is palpable in that one would think children would empathize, yet instead the opposite of that is what is displayed outwardly often happens.

Talking to the School

It cannot be emphasized enough that in all cases of bullying, it is important to report it to the school immediately. It is critical to report these incidences, especially if your child is LGBT. With rates of almost nine out of ten LGBT children bullied, chances are greater that a perceived homosexual or stated homosexual child is bullied. Of all reported suicide cases in children, as many as 30% of them are thought to be LGBT children. We, as a country, not just as parents, need to stop this trend in its tracks.

We have said before, and will say repeatedly, report bullying early, address it comprehensively, and get leaders involved. When a light is shone on this behavior, and it is made clear it is not acceptable, bullies will back down. Remember all the law enforcement, legal and community options available (see Chapters Four and Five).

As in all cases of bullying, your child has a right to be safe while at school. The school is responsible, under the Safe School Act of 1994, to be safe, free of drugs, and violence, and is obligated to provide a disciplined environment conducive to learning. If your child is harassed at school for any reason, the school is responsible for protecting your child under this Act.

Schools also have an obligation under Title IX to prohibit sex and gender discrimination. The federal law does not specifically ban discrimination based on sexual orientation, gender identity or gender expression, but it does forbid harassment directed at a LGBT student that is sexual in nature. If the school does not protect your child from harassment, consider filing a claim with The Office for Civil Rights at the Department of Education. The Department of Education takes cases of bullying seriously, and urges schools to do the same by sending letters to schools with examples of bullying, including the bullying of LGBT children. If your school does not take action, once you suggest that you will be filing a claim, the Office for Civil Rights at the Department of Education will take your case and discuss the school's inaction directly with them.

Reporting to the Office for Civil Rights at the Department of Education

Filing a claim with The Office for Civil Rights at the Department of Education is simple and straightforward. They have employees available to help you through the process. You do need to file a claim quickly as the department only allows 180 calendar days after an incident of discrimination to submit the complaint. Contact the office directly or file a claim online. The claimant will then receive a letter in the mail, a telephone call, or email stating that the complaint was received, and the next steps will be outlined. The conversation via telephone will consist of fact-finding. The Office for Civil Rights at the Department of Education will remain neutral during this process. They will contact the school to discuss the situation. In many cases, this contact with the school is enough for school administrators to update policies and procedures involving incidents of bullying.

HELPING YOUR CHILD

Most harassed LGBT children need love and support. The bullying they may receive on a daily basis is painful. Any assistance a child is given will help him feel more comfortable about who he is, and as a result, live a better life. Discuss with your child what to say to a bully, so he is prepared. Devise a game plan for the time he is in school each day. Role-play *comebacks* and options, such as walk with a crowd, sit near the school bus driver, and never take short cuts home.

The goal is to empower children so they do not live in fear. Encourage children to tell a trusted adult as soon as an incident occurs. Request they tell you each, and every, time they are harassed so that you can talk through their feelings. Explain to your child why it is important to report an incident to the school, and that the school has an obligation to keep them safe.

If your child shows signs of stress and does not want to go to school, or shows signs of depression such as sleeping too much or avoids participation in any activities, find ways to overcome these feelings so he can learn to cope with the situation. Seriously consider a therapist or counselor for your child, sooner rather than later. There are free counselors at many community centers. A trained therapist can be extremely helpful.

Another critical step is to find groups and organizations where your child is accepted. Do whatever it takes to find your child a place, or group, that embraces him and helps him feel comfortable. This may be an academic organization, a creative group, a volunteer social service, a book club, a church club, a musical group, a sports team, or an outdoor club. Get creative and find a place for your child to belong and fit in.

Finding a LGBT parent organization may help you relieve stress as well. Talking it out with other parents in the same situation may spark ideas of ways to help your child and yourself. If your child makes any comment about wanting to hurt himself or someone else, take it very seriously. A health care professional may need to evaluate the situation. Do not wait. Remember that LGBT children commit 30% of all youth suicides every year.

The following web sites are available to learn more:

- www.glaad.org
- www.hcsm.org
- www.nmha.org

LESSONS LEARNED

- Act fast. Contact the school.

- Do not accept "no" from your school on any level.

- Report bullying and get it stopped early. This is the key to success. The longer it goes on, the more powerful it becomes.

- Become informed and understand your rights. Provide your school with copies of laws, social service agency forms, and other materials. These are particularly effective visual aids when talking to the school administration.

- Consider getting an order of protection against key bullies. This can be filed in your county government building, and typically only takes a couple of weeks to implement.

- With civil rights violations, make sure you involve the superintendent right away.

- Ask the school for a plan and be an active part of the plan to solve the problem comprehensively. Do not accept "no." Ask for a timeline and make the school adhere to it.

- Civil rights attorneys provide free advice in most counties in the U.S. Use them.

- Report the issue to The Office for Civil Rights at the Department of Education if the school does not act.

- If there are signs of depression, or your child suggests harming himself or someone else, get counseling for your child quickly.

- Get support from GLBT parent organizations.

CHAPTER EIGHT
CARING FOR YOUR BULLIED
CHILD AND YOUR FAMILY

Most parents would probably say that caring for a bullied child centers on loving them and protecting them. If only it were as simple as that. Until you have been in a situation where your child has been tormented, either moderately or severely over an extended period, it is difficult to imagine how complex the support needs are for that child. Of course, lots of love will get your child through this period and beyond it.

But layered above that foundation of love is an intricate web of improving their self-esteem, distracting them from the negative, helping them feel safe, empowering them, and assisting them with new friends and interests. Equally important is to ensure they do not become overly cynical about people or become hyper-paranoid. This mission is particularly challenging when you, as a parent, are giving yourself the very same pep talk everyday.

That aside, if your child is being bullied, he needs you now, perhaps more than ever. Embrace the challenge. Equally important, accept the fact that he will need a little more attention than the rest of your family and let yourself be okay with that. You will be amazed how your family will be fine if you either let them help, or let them do a little extra to ensure your home stays whole and happy.

WHERE TO START: MORE "I LOVE YOU"

It seems ridiculously simple and obvious, but it really does work if you say, "I love you" regularly. If you do not already say those simple words every day to your child before he leaves for school, make sure you start. In addition to saying it more, say it with meaning. Make sure you hug and kiss your child more. Now, some teenagers will find this irritating, but try to find a tactile gesture that will not embarrass or agitate them.

THIRD PARTY VALIDATION OF YOUR CHILD'S SELF-WORTH

Another important thing you can do to help a child feel loved, and not just by the family, is to mention that other adults have said many times that they *really respect you.* Other compliments can focus on a child's strength of character, great personality, attractiveness, intellect, and talent. It can be a teacher, neighbor, coach, counselor or friend's parent who bestow the compliment. It can be anybody your child reveres in some way. Mention the compliment in passing, nonchalantly; make it sound like an item you may have forgotten to pass on earlier, but have now remembered.

Children, particularly from 9 to 17 years of age, feel most confident about themselves when their peers either admire them or respect them. Equally important, the opinions of adults they respect or admire are helpful when rebuilding your child's self-esteem. When your child is feeling down about himself, remind him of the various adults and children who respect him or find him bright, interesting, talented, funny or good-looking. Most bullied children feel they do not measure up, and at worst, begin to lose all self-respect. When I hear about children feeling horrible and negative about themselves due to a bully's actions, it really makes my blood boil. No one should have the power to do something so negative to a child.

Anecdote: Not long before we started this book, a mother in another town called me. A neighbor had referred her. She was obviously upset. Her daughter, Tina, 15 years old, was on the volleyball team and was a fair player, but not a star. Additionally, she was extremely shy and found it hard to perform in public during games. Tina loved volleyball and worked hard, but was not a starter for the team. During a recent game, however, she had an opportunity to play when one of the starters got hurt.

Unfortunately, Tina missed a ball in the final seconds of the game, and the team lost. In the locker room, the star player walked over to her and said in a chastising voice, "You stupid bitch. Not only are you a loser, but you are fat, and the worst volleyball player we have ever had on the team. You ruined everything for this whole team. I hope you are happy." With that, she turned away, and the rest of the team either followed her or ignored the scene.

Tina's mother explained that this behavior happened regularly with a group of girls reacting in one of two ways to Tina. They either completely ignored her, or talked about her online and called her horrible names. Tina's mother asked me what to do beyond providing love and respect at home. I suggested she help Tina realize that many people outside the home love and respect her. More importantly, she should help Tina understand that her peers think she is talented and need to let her know that. If you have to go out and find this information or make it up, remind your bullied child that several people admire her. In Tina's case, her mother should talk with the coach and ask him to praise Tina regularly. Without embarrassing Tina, a teammate should be identified that will provide Tina with non-patronizing support as well. This will be very credible to Tina.

FINDING NEW FRIENDS AND INTERESTS

Often assisting your child to find new friends will accomplish two things. One, it will keep the child distracted from the day-to-day bullying. Two, it will ultimately, help him learn greater social skills. Of course, this is not easy, but you will find it is worth the effort. Note: frequently, after a child has been bullied for a while, he needs a social break for a few weeks. Let the child have this space if wanted, but watch him closely for signs of depression. As stated previously, do not ignore signs of depression; get professional help.

So where are new friends, interests, and hobbies found? Again, it sounds overly simplistic, but your child should make a list of kids and interests he has never pursued before. Help your child with this. The following are some questions that will help him identify those friends and activities.

FINDING NEW FRIENDS

1. Who are the children you see at school, or at other activities, that seem nice or interesting, but who you have never talked to or approached?

2. Is there anybody in any of your classes who talks to you sometimes, but that you do not really know?

3. Is your bully tormenting anybody else? Maybe you should team up with the other child who is bullied and support each other?

4. Is there anybody outside of school that you have met that you think you would like to know better?

FINDING NEW ACTIVITIES

1. Visit a neighboring town and get activity catalogs at other park districts, community colleges, and other municipally based resources, to explore new activities with new children.

2. Make a list of things your child has never tried such as snowboarding, playing an instrument, volunteering, joining a club, playing a new sport, additional classes at park districts and community centers, crafts, collector's clubs, group volunteer programs, church youth groups, ski and skating clubs, swim clubs, and YMCA activities.

3. Google activities in your community relative to your child's list of interests, and investigate the results.

INSULATING YOUR CHILD FROM FURTHER BULLYING

Some children who have been bullied, but certainly not all, were tormented because the bullies wanted to get a reaction. Some bullies are empowered to bully further when a child over-reacts; some bullies are incited when a child ignores them. This is where role-playing with your child is extremely helpful.

Work with your child to develop strategies, approaches, responses and comebacks. As we have mentioned before, ignoring bullying once can put a stop to a rude behavior, but if it continues, your child should address it.

Sometimes a funny and biting comment back will prevent more agitation. But sometimes, it requires other tools like a humorous comment, a look or a nod. Every child is different and should do what suits them well. When I was young, I felt sarcasm worked, but that response may not be comfortable for many children.

Role play a variety of options with your child and practice them.

You may want to consider the following complimentary or inexpensive resources in your community.

1. YMCAs and community clubs have groups that help children with social skills. Participants are generally eight to 15 years of age who just need a little practice overcoming awkward or shy behaviors that bullies target.

2. Some schools have children's groups that meet with a counselor each week and monthly to discuss social challenges or issues. A peer group helps children solve challenges with real world skills, ideas and strategies. Note: you can always ask your school counselor or psychologist to start a group if one currently does not exist. As always, do not take "no" for an answer, but be willing to help that professional start the group and keep it active.

3. Many local child therapists or psychologists facilitate groups focusing on social skills challenges. Again, Google is your friend here.

TALK ABOUT FEELINGS WHENEVER YOU FEEL YOU HAVE AN OPENING

Not all children want to talk about their feelings, but whenever they start to talk, put your very best listening and non-judgmental face on. It is important for children to know you will listen. Between the ages of eight to 11 years of age, they tend to want answers. After 11 years of age, they just want to vent. Respect these differences. Try not to judge, but ask them to share their feelings.

When your child makes a comment such as, "I wish that bully would die." or "I want to smash that kid's face in.", let your child know that these feelings are normal. In fact, tell your child how healthy it is to have these feelings. Those feelings only become unhealthy when you act on them. Remind your child that if he hurts somebody, then he could be considered a bully. Do not let the bullies have this type of satisfaction. If the aggressive feelings become constant, please seek professional help for your child.

A Very Dicey Topic: Fighting Back

Wow, this is a very individualized choice. We have told our kids that you absolutely must fight back and defend yourself. If someone physically hits you, push them away first. If they don't stop, fight back. Some will disagree with us and we respect that perspective. But at the end of the day, from practical experience, it works. If your child is much smaller, running works or getting helps work too.

Caring for Your Family During This Time

There will be some natural tension in the house when a child is bullied outside the home. Try to alleviate the tension, and distract your family whenever possible.

Good Tricks for the Whole Family

1. Rent comedy movies and watch them as a family.

2. Become more physically active. Play sports together, walk together, play catch, go swimming, ice-skating, bike riding, or go to the gym. Just get moving several times a week.

3. See your extended family more so that the child can play with others without the baggage. It will allow you also, as parents, to vent to another person the child is close to and get another opinion.

4. Try to set up dates with other families that are trusted. This allows children to be social with "safe kids".

Be On Alert

If you do not already have parental controls on your computer, get them. It is important to have as many positive influences as possible. Look at the browser history on your computer frequently to ensure your child is not looking for "dark solutions" on the Internet. There are many troubled folks in the world, and we do not want your child to get any ideas from them.

Similarly, watch your child's phone call, text and social media history on all the devices he uses. Make sure that there is not any tormenting going on, and make sure he is not planning anything with anybody that will get him into trouble. See Chapter 15 on social media to learn more on this topic.

SPOUSAL TENSION

A sensitive topic is spousal tension. Frequently, spouses will disagree on approaches to the bullying. Throughout this time of anxiety, it is likely, and we have experienced this ourselves. There will at least be occasional disagreements. One spouse will want an aggressive approach; the other will want a softer version. Alternately, one will want to stick their head in the sand completely, and the other wants to take action.

This is all common. One thing you must know. The longer you ignore bullying, the longer it goes on. There are times when a bully will get bored and move on, but the damage is done. Therefore, for spouses who do not want to rock the boat, or who are embarrassed, remember that if the situation does not go away within a few weeks, it will keep going and worse. It will become acceptable throughout the community to bully your child. Other children will see it, and will either try bullying your child or simply support the bully.

Advice to the spouse that does not want to act: put your child first and think about your child's feelings and emotional well-being. Be brave and do not worry about the wagging fingers and tongues in your community. We think you will make the right choice. Make sure that you carry on normally as a family, so your bullied child does not feel pitied or viewed with a microscope.

Now, this may make for some tension in your marriage. We know. Try to talk about it when the more assertive spouse has solutions to offer. Talking about it repeatedly without providing solutions becomes destructive. Try to divide and conquer when solving the problem. Individually find solutions and come together again to discuss and assess. Compromise. Listen. Above all else, make sure you are putting your child first. Do not belittle your spouse's objections. Rather, make certain you identify the good points they have made. Revise the plan together. Be a team. Remind each other that you are a team!

LESSONS LEARNED

- Make sure everyone in the family boosts your bullied child's confidence, frequently.

- Find ways for peers or adults that your child respects to share their admiration for your child with them.

- Ensure your child retains friends throughout the bullying solution.

- Help your child find new interests and activities.

- Assist your child in making new friends through new clubs, groups or activities.

- If you see signs of depression or anxiety, get your child professional help with a counselor or therapist.

- Take advantage of both school counselors and psychologists.

- If your child could use help with social skills, find therapists or community centers that have social skill development groups.

- Do more family activities. Stay active and distract your bullied child as much as possible away from negativity.

- Love your child, build confidence. Repeat.

CHAPTER NINE
CONSEQUENCES OF INACTION
BY THE FAMILY OF THE BULLY

REACTION FROM THE BULLY'S FAMILY

We have spent a fair amount of time talking to bully's parents and families. We have seen many different reactions. A very upset mother of a once popular female bully once contacted us. Her child was now ostracized and isolated from her friends because she was a bully. She believed her daughter's situation was our fault and that her child was no longer popular because we pushed our schools into creating anti-bullying policies. Many families of bullies cannot believe their child is bullying and cannot believe that their child would do anything to deliberately harm another person. If we had a nickel for every time we have heard, "Not my child!", we would be incredibly wealthy. Even when presented with undeniable evidence that their child was bullying, parents will make excuses and say things like, "Oh well, my child had a bad day.", or "He did not mean it the way it sounded." There are few cases where this is actually true.

Sometimes bullying behavior is learned at home. Sometimes bullies learn how to bully from their own parents or the media. Parents of bullies can be manipulative. We've seen many situations where the parents of the bully turn the situation around and make it as if the victim was truly the bully. Similarly, parents of bullies will defend their children and say that it was two-sided. This does happen. Parents of victims should make certain their own child did not bully as well. Make it clear that the bullying started with the other child, if in fact, that is true. Do not be manipulated, but be objective.

On rare occasions have we seen parents be apologetic and share the specific actions they will take to end the bullying. The majority of parents of the bully, at the very least, suspect their child is bullying. However, more often than not, they cannot admit it even to themselves. They often tend to do nothing until forced to do so by the school, law enforcement, or a lawsuit brought upon by the victim's family.

61

CONSEQUENCES OF INACTION

If you ignore the problem, it will not go away and it will only become worse. The consequences of inaction by the bully's family are multifold. There is continued harm to the victim. Bullying is getting an enormous amount of attention by the media and this could bring on embarrassment to the bully's family. The victims and their families are no longer being a doormat and are starting to make a lot of noise. There has been an increase in legal action taken by families of victim's against the families of bullies. Around the age of 14, the bully stops gaining popularity and friends of bullies tend to distance themselves. As children get older and they have been bystanders, some do begin to take action to stop the bully.

Long-term effects of being a bully are just as dangerous as the long-term effects on a victim. Bullies become angry adults with very few, if any, close relationships. Alcoholism, drug abuse, personality disorders, anxiety and depression are common among adults that bullied as children. Even more alarming is that 60% of those who bullied usually pass through the criminal justice system by 24 years of age. Bullies in the work place often lose their jobs, and are unemployed or unemployable. It is important to take action if your child is a bully because they will not get better until they stop bullying.

WHAT TO DO IF YOU SUSPECT YOUR CHILD IS BULLYING

- Continually watch how your child interacts and communicates with other children and adults. Does your child treat others with respect? Does he like to be dominant? Does he blame others for his problems? Is he intolerant of differences? If you suspect that your child has been showing bully-like tendencies, ask your child if he has ever humiliated or embarrassed another child. If he says yes, have an open dialogue about why he did it. If he says no, have an open discussion about bullying and the consequences associated with bullying.

- Check e-mail, texts, Facebook pages, and the history on the computer and see how your child interacts with others. Do not feel that this is an invasion of privacy since you most likely own the equipment. Listen to your child as he talks to friends on the telephone. Listen to what they are saying and how they are saying it. Without calling them bullies, point out any bully-like behaviors, and firmly tell them it is not acceptable. It is important to point out and praise empathetic and kind behaviors that will encourage respectful interaction with others. If the disrespectful pattern of behaviors continues, take away privileges, such as cell phones and Internet use for non-school activities until the child can manage the technology with respect. Help the child reflect on his actions, and learn how to be positive.

- If your child is bullying, and uses video games, remove the games until he earns the privilege by showing respectful behavior. It is likely your child will put up an enormous fight because technology has become an integral part of his life. Without it, he feels lost. Do not allow or accept bullying behavior towards you, the parent. It is important, yet difficult, to stay strong. It is easier to ignore the behavior and allow it to happen. This will only cause you more pain and anguish in the future. You do not want your child incarcerated or in a treatment facility for drug and alcohol abuse. Let it be known that there are new rules around disrespectful behavior in your home. You will be monitoring the child's activities at school, and online, in order to ensure respectful behavior. It is better to address the situation before it becomes a problem.

- If you receive a call from the school, or a victims' parents, stating that your child has been participating in bully-like behaviors, it is important for you not to jump to the child's defense or to make excuses for your child's behavior. It is best for everyone to solve this problem quickly. Ask for a meeting with the child's teachers and principal without the child being present. This will allow for an open discussion without fear of humiliating your child. Take notes and request a second meeting after you speak to your child. After the meeting, address the situation calmly and in a non-confrontational manner with your child. Ask a few open ended questions, and let your child speak. Take notes so that you can refer back to them if needed.

- If you do find your child was disrespectful to another child, consider having your child formally apologize to the victim and the victim's family. Being accountable is critical when reforming the behavior. The child must admit the behavior, and devise a plan to make amends. It is the right thing to do to teach your child a lesson and allow the victim's family to heal. This act of true humility should be the last interaction your child has with the victim. Instruct your child not to discuss the situation with any of their friends.

- If your child continues to bully, seek professional help. Bullies need as much help, and sometimes more, as the victim. Changing behavior that has become a habit, such as bullying, takes work, and therapy is helpful. Do not ignore the signs. The school and your state should have a social worker that can help you find professional help.

LESSONS LEARNED

- Do not ignore the situation. It will only get worse.

- Be accountable and force the bully to be accountable.

- Find solutions, not excuses for the behavior.

- Create rules regarding respect in your home.

- Seek professional help if needed.

CHAPTER TEN
MOTIVATIONS FOR BULLYING

When a child is bullied, one of the first questions parents ask is, "Why my child?" There are many reasons a bully engages is this behavior, and sometimes there is no reason at all. Years ago, people would say that bullies were insecure, had self-esteem issues, or had depression problems. The bully was motivated by inner anger and hatred toward others. In some cases, this is still true, but today's bullies have higher self-esteem, and are viewed by friends as popular and influential. His peers find them amusing, so the more he teases and torments, the more entertaining he is to adoring pals, which, in turn, motivates the bully to continue. Adults sometimes view today's modern bully as charming, polite and even witty because the bully is well rehearsed on how to act in front of an adult. Teachers often cannot believe these seemingly model children are bullies since they are so well liked at school. The parents of the bully deny that their child could ever do anything wrong, but is certainly "not their perfect angel."

So why do children bully? What is the motivation behind bullying? There may be a combination of motives. A few common traits bullies seem to share are a lack of empathy and the inability to tolerate differences in humans. They also are rather crafty, well-practiced liars, and know when to bully so they are not caught. If they are caught they can usually talk their way out of it with a perfectly logical explanation, making it seem as if the victim is overly sensitive or simply misunderstood. The most common motive behind bullying is that the bully gets his or her peers to laugh while making fun of someone else. Being funny makes them popular. Alternatively, simply having power to judge another child makes the bully feel popular and revered. Let's review some classic motives behind bullying.

POWER AND CONTROL

A narcissistic personality puts people down in order to feel better about himself. He is in charge; he is the boss, the leader, the number one. He does not want anyone as a co-leader or even a close second. He does want, however, followers and supporters of his actions. This child is the one who is in control of who sits at the lunch table, who is picked first on the kickball team at recess, and who controls the selection of those allowed to be in the walking home club. This child often witnesses acts of bullying at home. A mother or father who mistreats their spouse, their children and/or co-worker, acts as a negative role model for their child. This bully is motivated by the need to be the most powerful and in control. He often turns on children within his group if they snub the leader or are a threat to his power.

JEALOUSY

Children often bully another child because they are jealous of them. Maybe one girl is now dating the other girl's former boyfriend, or a boy has more cool stuff than the bully does. Similarly, the bully may have a personal vendetta for something that accidentally happened on the ball field several years prior. The jealous bully tends to be the over indulgent child who has very few boundaries, or rules at home, and lacks adult supervision. This bully is motivated by jealousy, and often spreads rumors about the victim to ensure the victim is negatively perceived by other children, and, even adults.

BULLIES CANNOT SEEM TO ACCEPT LGBT CHILDREN

Lesbian, gay, bisexual, transgender (LGBT) children are bullied at alarming rates. There are varieties of motives behind bullying LGBT children. Most often incidents are sparked by the bully's own misguided beliefs, or the beliefs of their misguided parents. These children hold the belief that being LGBT is wrong, and that the LGBT child has the ability to be straight, but for some reason, chooses another lifestyle. This is made worse in small, conservative towns where it is discussed openly at churches where a pastor's interpretation of the bible facilitates judgment of LGBT people. The inability to accept differences, and the wish to force the beliefs on others, motivates the bully to continue.

WEIGHT ISSUES

Overweight children are bullied at equally high rates as lesbian and gay children. The bully often thinks of these children as an "easy target". It is a visual difference, and seemingly easier for the bully to make disrespectful and hurtful jokes about the victim. This bully is motivated by the need to be funny, and the center of attention, in a cruel and demeaning way.

SPECIAL NEEDS CHILDREN

Walking down the hall, the bully makes a soft, disrespectful remark behind the back of a hearing-impaired child just to get a laugh. Another child makes a comment that he knows is going to upset a little girl that is mentally disabled just to see her cry. A girl dares another girl to trip a child who has a physical disability. Motivated by being funny, and getting a thrill out of being disrespectful to a child with special needs, is sadly a common activity in our schools today.

RELIGION

Name any faith, and children will make fun of it or demean it, simply because it is not their own faith. Children of the Muslim faith are often called terrorists, or teased because of food restrictions. Jewish children are questioned as to why they were able to miss school because of a holiday that was not celebrated by the bully. Bullies will make a joke that Santa does not visit the homes of Seventh Day Adventist children because, "He does not like them." These are all motives based on intolerance of differences.

RACE

While we have made progress in racial acceptance, bullies have not gotten this message. One would think that with the diversity in the world, this would be outdated. Just as in the 1950's and 1960's, children still sometimes react negatively to the color of a person's skin. It really is unfortunate in our fourth decade after the civil rights movement, that children of today do not simply accept everyone. Since children with similar backgrounds tend to stick together, children are often bullied in groups. Cultural differences such as what they eat for lunch or how they dress, spur ongoing comments from bullies. The bully is motivated by his own insecurities and the inability to accept differences in other children. Sadly, racism is often a trait that is learned at home, or frequently, joked about on television and in video games. Both television and video games are major influences on our children today.

RANDOMLY CHOSEN OR NO REASON AT ALL

The victim child was in the right place at the wrong time. The child is not particularly different other than he is not part of the group. The bully is motivated by an opportunity to bully.

How dull would it be if we all looked and acted like Barbie and Ken? A loner, a quiet child, a bright and gifted child who perhaps is more interested in academics than socializing, the non-athlete, the smaller child, the kid with family problems are often targets. It can be for any reason, or no reason at all. Older children bullying a younger child to get a reaction, such as tears or simply to induce fear, happens regularly. We could go on and on stating reasons why bullies bully. Not a single one of them are a good reason to bully. How dull would it be if we all looked and acted like Barbie and Ken? For the bully, any difference is a good reason to bully. Most bullies are motivated by a need to be powerful and in control. They lack empathy and like to be the class clown. Parents of bullied children understand that there is never a valid reason to bully. Never.

A Bright By-Stander

We were able to witness an unbelievable act of kindness by a by-stander during an end-of-school field day event. A group of children, both boys and girls, were yelling at a special needs child on their team for being slow during one of the races. There was no score recorded officially by the teachers but the children knew who was going to get bragging rights for winning the most events. J.J., a by-stander, told the unkind children who were demeaning the special needs child to sit down and be quiet. J.J. was able to get a group of his friends on their feet cheering while he helped the child finish the race. This was a heart-warming act of kindness by J.J. The teacher pointed out the act of kindness to the principal who called J.J.'s parents, and all the children assisting the child, to compliment them on a truly kind and respectful act. When we talked to the mother of J.J. about the incident, she said, "I expect nothing less than kindness from him". A positive parental expectation J.J. was able to share with his friends. And, he will be that way for life.

Lessons Learned

- Remind your child that it is the bully who has the issue, not the victim.
- Discuss differences in children and tell your child that it is okay to be unique. Not everyone has to be the same.
- Encourage kindness and compliment other acts of kindness.
- Remind children that it is okay to joke and tease, just make certain it will not be offensive to anyone.

CHAPTER ELEVEN
WHY IS BULLYING SUCH A PROBLEM?

It is a big question, and, there are many answers. There is not one, singular source for this societal problem. Many would like to blame the schools. Some would like to blame parents. Still others think the media and entertainment companies are at fault. The real answer? It is all of the above. In the simplest of terms, bullying has become a distinct problem because it has become accepted, and acceptable, for our children to be disrespectful to one another in our communities. Let us break it down by the primary influencers of our children.

PARENTS

Each parental generation reacts to the generation before them. In many ways this is an effective way to continually improve our parenting abilities in the human race. However, sometimes as a generation, we go to the opposite end of the continuum from the generation before us, and those extreme shifts usually present new problems.

As an example, the parents before us tended to be more authoritative in their children's lives and did not become as engaged in every detail of their lives. Of course, there are exceptions to this generalization. Conversely, the current generation becomes over-involved in some ways, and at times, prioritizes being friends with their children instead of being the parent. Again, only true for some of the people, some of the time, but enough so that it has contributed heavily to the unfortunate acceptance of bullying as some rite of passage in childhood. As we say repeatedly, bullying is not acceptable, and should not be accepted as a necessary part of childhood.

Because of parents' zeal to be liked, and thought of as a friend by their child, parents have stopped imparting real consequences with teachable moments to their children. Consequences help us learn, reflect and introspect. Without consequences, we tend to begin to think we are invincible and can "do whatever we want." It is then natural for some of our children to feel entitled and act as if they are beyond the laws of civility and society.

Additionally, many parents seem to prioritize popularity for their children over all else, as the most important thing in their lives. It is clear with this generation that, either consciously or unconsciously, parents are communicating the supreme importance of popularity. This results in children doing whatever it takes to achieve popularity. The heartbreak here is that these children translate the need and importance of popularity into judging and criticizing other children so they look more interesting, attractive, more in the know, and "cooler". The need for popularity is the number one driver for bullying.

Similarly, many parents today forget that empathy needs to be taught. While many children are born with it, some need to be taught how to empathize, or at the very least, it needs to be cultivated. This is not easy, but a necessary role for a parent. Unfortunately, when children do not receive consequences and are not taught to empathize, they become un-accepting of others and cannot relate to all types of people and personalities. Finally, many parents ignore bullying behavior and call it "kids being kids." Sometimes it really is "kids' stuff." Sometimes, it is not! If the behavior goes unchecked in a child that is not empathetic, it quickly turns into bullying. Sadly in its totality, there are some parents who create the perfect recipe for a bully.

Invincibility + low/no empathy + ignored, unchecked behavior = Bully

SCHOOLS

Schools, to a certain degree, are in a difficult situation. They are charged with teaching and caring for our children several hours per day. They often complain that they barely have enough time for basic curriculum. While there is a wide body of developmental and educational research indicating that social emotional learning is critical for a child's development, both academically and emotionally, it seems to receive little attention. Only the most progressive schools have embedded social emotional learning in their curriculum. Most school districts feel they will get strong resistance from their parents if they attempt to give social emotional learning its due in the average day of each child.

Another issue is that many parents simply do not believe bullying is a problem. In fact, if your child is not being bullied, it probably does not even enter most parents' consciousness. While there are shining examples of school districts that have strong social emotional learning programs embedded, and effective anti-bullying programs, many others do not have these types of programs in place.

To make matters worse, our children are less empathetic and less accountable than the generation before them.

Combine all of this, and schools are in a demanding place. They begin to be in bully-triage mode frequently. The school is busy addressing acute issues and finds it is difficult to present real, authentic bully prevention programs because of time and resource issues.

We as parents should not accept, "It is what it is." Schools need to step up now! If children are not learning social emotional skills, such as empathy, tolerance and celebrating differences at home, the schools need to fill that gap, and quickly. If they do not, this generation, and the next, will be in a precarious situation.

As a nation, we have dropped in the area of education levels from 9th in the world in the 1980's to 25th place in 2009 among all advanced nations. This is absurd in a nation of resources such as the U.S. This is the very best way to become less competitive as a nation in a very competitive world. However, let us connect the dots here. When children are not comfortable because they do not feel safe and feel they are judged, of course, they will not learn well. Clearly, bullying is a contributing factor to children's education levels dropping precipitously.

COMMUNITIES

Culpability for bullying is really everywhere is society. There are definitely communities that do not allow it; there are communities who are unaware it exists; and, most unfortunately, there are those communities who actually foster bullying. Communities tend to have personalities. Highly competitive communities, this can be at any socio-economic level, not just the wealthy or well-educated, are among the worst offenders. In these highly competitive communities, either sports excellence or academic excellence is revered and becomes a "take no prisoners" type of attitude that prevails at all ages. Because of the intense pressure to achieve in sports or academics, children typically try to make other children look inadequate in order to diminish their self-esteem and make themselves look and feel better. Bullies will do this to those children who pose a threat to their status or standing. Or, will act this way toward just about anyone, even those who pose no threat to their status, in order to feel powerful and superior. In turn, this behavior becomes accepted and coined as *healthy competition*. While this term can be appropriate and useful, this type of competition is far from healthy. When it becomes a power and control issue, it becomes very unhealthy.

Another very unhealthy attitude in some communities is lack of acceptance of cultural, religious, skin color or sexuality differences. When children learn from their role models—parents, teachers, coaches, mentors, older children—not to accept others based on race, culture, religion or sexuality, they clearly will follow and emulate that hateful behavior. Yes, this Neanderthal behavior is still alive and well. This is how bullying becomes accepted and almost desirable behavior in some communities.

THE PARADIGM NEEDS TO CHANGE

As you can see, there are many contributing factors and reasons why bullying has become a widespread problem. The paradigm where popularity is critical at any cost, or the lack of acceptance of others prevails, prevents our children from evolving into a better generation than we are. Do we want this generation to be the first generation that does not evolve socially, emotionally and mentally better than the generation before it? It is likely to happen if we do not change attitudes, and do it quickly.

LESSONS LEARNED

- Teach your children, and all children, empathy whenever you can.

- Teach your children, and all children, to celebrate our differences and not criticize or judge differences.

- Help your children understand popularity is not important, but being a good person and doing the right thing are very important in life.

- Some competition is good, but it can grow to unhealthy levels.

- Be a role model and leader of acceptance and empathy in your community.

- We, as a society, have to change the paradigm that bullying is somehow acceptable to being unacceptable.

CHAPTER TWELVE
THE IMPACT OF BULLYING
ON A CHILD AND ITS
LASTING EFFECTS

There is no doubt why bullying has become such an epidemic. Our children are bombarded with shows depicting bad behavior. Shows such as "Mean Girls", and all the reality TV shows with young adults being nasty and rude to one another, are examples. Then there are the political smear campaigns that bully each other in front of their own children. I cannot even have the news on when my children are in the room since the television is filled with images of young people killing one another to demonstrate their power. What are they teaching our children? That it is okay to be cruel, nasty, rude, disrespectful, and abusive? No thank you. That is not the behavior I want my children to model. Whatever happened to the Cosbys? The Waltons? They were always kind and respectful to one another. How about "Leave It To Beaver"? Sure, 'The Beav' made a few mistakes, but he was not trying to hurt people intentionally. The "Brady Bunch" portrayed positive images of stepsiblings caring for each another. All I know is if I bullied someone as a child, my parents would have grounded me for a month, and if I did it again, it would be two months to life. In fact, if I found one of my children to be bullying, acting rudely, harassing or abusing someone they would be told to immediately apologize to the child and to their parents and be forced to perform some type of volunteer work. I would also take away their video games for a long time.

The lasting effects of bullying behavior can be felt for a lifetime. The good news is, with a little encouragement and a few action steps from loving parents and friends, this too shall pass. Getting to that level might feel like you are climbing Mount Everest, but it will pass! Being bullied is humiliating and isolating. I believe the reason why I was so insistent about nipping this bullying situation in the bud early with my son was because I was severely bullied as a child.

MY PERSONAL STORY (J.E. DIMARCO)

Growing up, my best friend, Suzie, and I were inseparable from kindergarten until the dreaded eighth grade. Sure we had our issues every now and again, but we were always best friends. We dressed the same; we played the same sports; we were both cheerleaders; we slept over each other's homes; and, we were as close any two girls could be.

At the age of 13 things took a horrible turn. I was having some problems at home; my parents were going through a grueling divorce, and I became somewhat introverted. Despite it all, my mom always said I was a very happy-go-lucky child and nothing ever seemed to bother me. Suzie, too, was having her problems at home. She lost her brother to cancer and her parents were understandably having some issues because of it. I think she was looking for attention and lashed out. Unfortunately, I was on the receiving end of her lashing out.

Early in the eighth grade, I became very ill with a severe case of pneumonia and was out of school for two weeks. I went back to school to find out that I had no friends. I had no idea why. I examined my behavior trying to decide if it was it something I did. Was it something that I didn't do? Was it something I said? Was it the way I dressed? I was beyond confused, and extremely sad. How could my best friend for practically my entire life not want to be my best friend anymore? What was even more confusing was trying to understand why all of my other girl friends were not speaking to me. At first, they were mean and then they treated me as if I was invisible.

At first, it was silly things like cruel telephone calls. Then it turned into 10 girls at once calling me unkind names in the cafeteria. Once, I was uninvited to sit with them at lunch, and one at a time, they would come up behind me and say something like, "Nobody likes you. You have ugly hair. You wear the same clothing over and over. Your eyebrows are too bushy." One time I just blew up and started screaming at them to leave me alone, which only prompted a roar of laughter. I ran out of the cafeteria, only to be reprimanded for yelling and leaving the area. Not too different from the mean girls we see today; however, it was not broadcast all over the internet or via text message. I never told my parents what was going on. I was so full of shame. I remember finding some new friends: food, sleep, running, and my dogs.

Food was my *drug* of choice, as it seemed to numb the pain temporarily. Chocolate, specifically, made me feel very happy for a while. Then it was cruel just like my friends. It gave me a sugar high followed by a sugar low. One time I was so sad after school that I ate an entire Sara Lee chocolate cake. My mother purchased it for a church outing and had it in the freezer. Yep, I even ate it frozen. I remember taking the first bite; it was so tasty and then a second bite and the third. I did not taste anything past the third bite; I think my taste buds were frozen. I continued to eat the entire frozen cake. When my mother was looking for it that night there was no way I was going to ever admit I ate the entire chocolate cake, as I did not want to risk my mom hating me too.

That lack of energy from the sugar low, that preceded the sugar high, introduced me to my next best friend, which was sleep. I slept all the time. I would get up late, go to bed early, and take naps during the day right after school. Sometimes I would fake being sick just to stay home from school to sleep. Ahhh, what a friend I had in my comforter. She, the comforter, was so nice. But my new friends betrayed me too. When my new friends, food and sleep got together, I got plump.

My eating and sleeping habits prompted my dad to take action by hiding all the sweets in our home. The cookie monster had taken over my body and my father was not fond of her. One night at dinner, he suggested I not have seconds since I was getting a little chubby. Great! Now, I am fat and have no friends. Despite his comments I did manage to find his beloved marshmallow cookies and polish them off. I knew he would be so angry with me if he found out I ate one let alone all 12 I devoured in one sitting, so I took off to the store to replace them. In one of my many trips to the grocery store to replace the treats, I decided to purchase some diet pills. That was back in the 1970s disco era when thin was in, and Dexatrim was the way to get there. The diet pills made me jittery and caused a rift with my best friend, sleep, who had already betrayed me. Since I could not sleep, I had to find yet another new best friend, running.

I once heard that all runners are running from something. In this case, I was definitely running from my pain. I would eat, and then I would sleep, and then go for a very long run. I never did get that infamous runner's high. When the weight would not come off, I resorted to starvation. I would not eat for days and just run and sleep. That made me even more depressed. I then would eat and sleep some more.

I think my real best friends, my dogs, saved my life. My beagles, named Woodstock and Marcie, thought I could do no wrong. They were always waiting for me at the door when I came home. They would eat with me, sleep with me, and run with me. I am really not sure what I would have done without them. They gave me the unconditional love that I needed during that time of my life. I was very fortunate to have them. Somehow they knew I was in pain and comforted me, by saying nothing and accepting me for me.

My mother would not have found out about what was going on at school had I not been caught ditching school. My mother was a schoolteacher so needless-to-say my education was extremely important to her. I had never ditched school before, and she knew that there had to be a good reason. My mother and I were always very close, even during those teen years. When I told her what was going on, she was crushed. I begged her not to do anything about the situation. I was too embarrassed, and I also did not want things to escalate at school. She thankfully did not listen to me. My mother is a kind, gentle person; however, when it came to her children, she is like a mother bear protecting her cubs. My mother immediately went to the school. She talked to the counselors, the dean, the principal and the teachers. Their suggestion was to bring it up at the school board. "The school board?" she thought. What are they going to do? She talked to the board, and they said "girls will be girls", and did nothing.

My mother's next step was to talk to my best friend, Suzie's, mother. Suzie's mother explained to my mother that their family was going through a very difficult time, and she did not want to talk to her husband about it. Instead, she would talk to Suzie and ask her to be friends with me again. This made the situation even worse. Suzie and the girls were even meaner, calling me names and pulling my hair in the bathroom. This went on for months before finally my mother decided I was going to go to a private high school the following year. I needed a fresh break, and she felt this was the best thing for me.

I was registered at the private high school, and, at the last minute, I decided that I was not going to let anyone dictate my future. I had enough. It was like I had an epiphany. My mother reluctantly agreed, and registered me at the public high school. We did agree that I would tell her everything no matter how small or trivial it seemed. On my first day of high school, I went in as if I owned the place. I had a new attitude, and I was not going to let anyone take me down. This was all an act because inside I was terrified I would never make any friends again. I did make new friends, even though at every social event I saw my former friends, which still hurt and made me feel ashamed. I felt ashamed for something that I never did or never said. Even at my 20th high school reunion, which I organized, I still felt a bit uncomfortable. How silly. Suzie was there, she gave me a gigantic hug, and it seemed that her own parenthood made her a much more compassionate and loving person. We spent several hours talking about our children, and all was right between us. Well, in some ways. She never apologized. Maybe she does not like to think about it either.

The sad thing about children that are bullied is that they do not always live up to their full potential as adults. Frequently, they have trouble trusting people, and they certainly do not stick their neck out for anything, for fear of being hurt or ridiculed by others. The consequences of being bullied as a child are strong. I still feel those wounds sometimes, even today. One of the consequences occurred in college. I did not want to get too close to too many people. College friends are some of the closest bonds people can share. I missed out on that experience. I reluctantly joined a sorority, Kappa Kappa Gamma, at the University of Illinois. That sorority had some of the most wonderful women the university had to offer—smart, fun, athletic, and responsible. I did not get close to many of those women because I was afraid of them. Most of them were wonderful, kind, and considerate, but I simply did not feel it was safe enough to test the water. It was much too soon to try, and I feared getting burned. I did not share much with them, but instead I called home every day and shared my day with my mother.

I still have issues trusting people. Whenever I meet someone new, I choose not to get too close to him, or her, or to say too much. I accept very few social invitations. I live in a town where women are very critical of one another. Topics of conversation frequently include who has what new thing, and who is wearing what new outfit– junior high stuff. I prefer to keep my distance with people. Yes, I do have a handful of very close friends who I trust. That trust is tested with them repeatedly. As part of that, I will share something with them to see how they will react, or I will say something critical about myself, and see how they respond. My mother always told me that you only need enough friends to count on one hand. She is right; however, there are many more good people in the world, who could make my life more colorful, if I would allow it. Yet, because of my childhood experience, I prefer "beige" friendships. I am very grateful for my handful of friends. They love me, for me, know my quirks, and are just fine with them.

EFFECTS ON A CHILD

Even after a bullying episode is over, and we hope for good, the lasting effects can be felt for years. It is almost easier to heal from a one-time, minor, physically abusive event, such as pushed down on the playground versus ongoing verbal abuse. If a child is called fat, ugly, stupid, or loser, repeatedly, they will internalize it and begin to believe it is true. This abuse can lead to eating disorders, self-mutilation, and severe depression, or at its worst, create suicidal tendencies. Even mild bullying can lead to self-doubt and low self-esteem. It is horrible that a bully has this type of control over another, and even more so, gets satisfaction from making someone miserable.

The humiliation and social isolation caused by a bully at a young age teaches children that others cannot be trusted and are hurtful. Even if a child was bullied by a mere acquaintance, building meaningful friendships can be difficult when the child does not know whom he can trust. The self-criticism and low self-esteem can also make a child uncomfortable in groups. They may tell themselves, "I am not good enough to play on this team. I am not good enough to play in the band, and I am not smart enough to play chess." As a result, children often prefer to be alone, refusing to join clubs or teams, unwilling to attend parties or social events, all leading to continual loneliness.

Fast-forward 10 years, assuming the bullied child did not receive therapy, or is still harboring anger and bitterness. It is now time for them to go off to college or enter the workplace. Trusting people, getting along with others, and working in teams is expected as we become adults. Relationships in both work and life become a challenge for a formerly bullied child. The same patterns of low self-esteem can lead to slow career advancement. It is reflected in their work. "I am not good enough to be a manager. I am not smart enough to learn that skill. Everyone likes *John*, and he will get the promotion." The self-loathing cycle continues.

In their personal lives, it is often difficult to find loving and caring companionship, since it is very hard to trust others, open up to friends, and function in social situations. The victims of bullying often have very little tolerance for flaws in friends or spouses. The littlest of quirks in people, such as talking too loudly or having too much fun at a social event, might be misconstrued as hurtful actions. A formerly bullied person feels those people "just want to be the life of the party and they are going to talk to everyone else but me." The bullied person quickly cuts off the person as a friend. Once again, trying to protect themselves by believing they are better off alone.

Some Lasting Effects of Being Bullied

- Anger, shame

- Fear, low self-esteem

- Poor grades

- Isolation, loneliness, sadness, and social anxiety

- Depression

- Eating Disorders

- Addictions

- Ability to trust diminished

- Difficulty making and keeping meaningful relationships

- Difficulties advancing in the work place

- Becomes totally risk-adverse

GOOD NEWS! IT CAN BE OVERCOME AND ADULTS CAN BE BETTER FOR IT!

The good news is that if you are an engaged and caring parent, you absolutely can help your child overcome this short-term obstacle in their lives. We know you can, because you have chosen to read this book, and possibly other materials to learn how to support your child. You are a wonderful parent. Remember that. Your child can flourish in life, and be even better, from the experience. Showing your child that he is loved, protected, and cared for is one of the best things that you can do for him. Undoing what the bully has done is possible. Encouraging relationships with friends; allowing children to come to your home rather than play at a park or public place; making sure the child has someone to walk to and from school with and have lunch with; and, many other safety nets will keep your child positive and help him get beyond the torment. Your school will have many resources to help your family. Talk to your child's teacher, school social worker, nurse, counselor and principal to see how they can help you help your child.

You might consider hiring a professional therapist. Do your homework to find a professional who deals with social isolation, anxiety, fear of relationships and with children who have been bullied. Interview several of them, and ask if they have experience helping children who have been bullied and what specifically they were able to accomplish with the child.

I wish I had a magic wand to make it all better for your family. Even as I am heavily involved in anti-bullying campaigns, I was unable to stop the same child from bullying my son over a two-year period. There had been a quiet period for my son for a while with no incidences, and then, out of the blue and with the start of sixth grade, it started again. Honestly, I could not believe that the same bully would start up again after being told multiple times by my son, as well as adults, to stop the disrespectful behavior. The parents of the bully have also been contacted, yet their son continues the abusive behavior to multiple children. I have learned that the best way to stop this is to act quickly and aggressively each and every time it happens. During our most recent incident, the school took action, and requested that the child not communicate with my son at all, and required that the parents and bully commit to this agreement. They have kept their commitment and life is better.

My husband and I are working hard to get our son "back". Each time we have an episode of bullying, he becomes more introverted, a little more self-conscious, and a little less happy. Since my son has made some good friends who know what has happened to him, they make sure friends at school, at social events and sports, surround him. Even though I have a full-time job, I volunteer every chance I can at school to make sure I am aware of what is going on. I observe and listen to what the kids are doing and saying. I have even asked my sisters and mother to fill in for me when I am unable to attend an event. I welcome his friends to hang out at our house, even if it means that my house is going to be a disaster. Again, it allows me to observe and listen to the kids. This information helps me better understand my son's situation and his school life.

Our parent group got together to discuss helping our children overcome the lasting effects of bullying. Everyone had a different idea, but the common theme was to be positive and loving while keeping life as normal as possible. No special games, toys or privileges; just a lot of love, praise and encouragement, but mostly love.

IDEAS ON HELPING A CHILD OVERCOME THE NEGATIVE EFFECTS OF BEING BULLIED

- Role-play with a child on how to say, "No! Stop it!" Say it aloud and with power. It can be cleansing.

- Reinforce to your child that this it is not his fault. There is nothing wrong with him. The bully has the problem.

- Encourage your child to walk with a group to, and from, school. Safety is in numbers.

- Suggest to your child that he sit with a friend near the driver on the bus.

- Urge your child to join a boys or girls club, perhaps in another town, to meet new friends.

- Become a parent volunteer at social events, school activities, a room parent and team parent.

- Invite children to play at your home. It will allow you time to observe and listen. Do not fret about the mess.

- Start a new hobby together or with a sibling or trusted friend. Always praise work well done.

- Join church youth groups. God can do powerful things for us.

- Ask for help from a school counselor, social worker and teachers.

- Seek professional help by a licensed therapist or social worker.

- Once your child is far beyond the pain, have them mentor a child who is being bullied to help them through it.

With a lot of love, and some guidance, your child will get through this. Your child has too much to offer the world. The bullies have done enough harm already. Do not let a bully take control of your child's life. Your child might be feeling hopeless and helpless. He does not have the wisdom to understand the situation will actually end. He might think he is the only one who has ever been bullied. Help him see the light at the end of the tunnel.

Remember, this too shall pass.

LESSONS LEARNED

- If your child is severely bullied, consider getting professional help, if possible. Do not let your child hinder his full potential in this world because of the bully.

- Ask for help from social workers and teachers at school.

- Encourage your child to meet new friends and try a new hobby or sport.

- Role-play with a child so that they can practice standing up for themselves.

- Take one day at a time. This too shall pass.

CHAPTER THIRTEEN
THE CONCEPT OF FRIENDSHIP
IN THIS GENERATION

Most would agree that the human race has evolved and become more sophisticated from generation to generation. This is good and not so good.
As we become more sophisticated as a society, we also learn how to
create more groups and more divisions. Certainly, we have become more accepting as a
whole, but we somehow still find ways to divide and judge.

When the current generation of parents were children, most struggled to be popular
or maintain popularity. Our parents did not necessarily tell us to try to be popular, but they
did not tell us not to. Some achieved high status; others did not. Judging others was
commonplace, and bullying was alive and well.

Now, with the current generation of children, parents have made it clear that being
popular *is important*. In fact, many parents consciously and unconsciously, guide their
children toward popularity, instead of individuality and independence of thought. As a
result, friendship is a more precarious proposition for the current generation. Loyalty is not
as important. Opportunism is revered, even rampant. Worst of all, staying away from
controversy is now critical. Parents teach their children to stay out of it. As a result, our
children do not understand that being a friend means standing up for each other and defending each other when a detractor demeans their friend. When we were children and a
friend, or anybody, was tormented, others would jump in and support the tormented child.
Today, this does not happen very often. This generation reveres popularity above all else,
even when faced with the ethical dilemma of defending a friend. They typically choose
popularity and avoiding controversy over friendship every time.

THE NEW GENERATION OF POPULAR

Parents are often consciously, or unconsciously, the driving force for a child to be
popular. Are they trying to fill a void they had as a child? Maybe they were one of the un-

cool, less popular, or maybe even bullied children? They understandably want more for their child. As an onlooker of the popular parent dance, it appears that parents of the semi-cool kids go out of their way to hang out with the parents of the cool kids so that their child is invited to all the popular activities. As we have learned from trying to *fix* our quiet, independent children to stand up for themselves, orchestrating their activities does not work. The wave of coolness changes from one day to the next with kids.

LIVING VICARIOUSLY THROUGH CHILDREN?

We often wonder if parents who push their children athletically are somehow living vicariously through their child's athletic performance. Have you ever witnessed a parent screaming at their child for a bad play on a ball field? Some parents often expect perfection from their child that often leads to a child who feels defeated by a less than stellar game. It is easily seen on the ball fields across the nation; parents fighting with a referee, their child's coach, or other parents over a wrong call in pee wee sports. One never knows if that bad call on an 8-year-old soccer player is going to cost their child a college scholarship and a chance for a career as a professional soccer player. What does this do to children? Children often lose the team spirit and pick on one kid to blame for the loss. Just as a parent yells at a child on a wrong play, a child often yells at another child for a mistake on the field.

MORE STUFF = MORE FRIENDS = CONDITIONAL FRIENDSHIPS

The parent, who buys their already overindulged, unappreciative child everything they could ever want because the neighborhood child has it, is everywhere. The latest and greatest toys, the finest clothing, and activities galore are the main operating systems today for parents. With this, often comes lack of structure in the household. Parents might be doing this because they feel that they did not have much as a child, which caused them not to have friends. They also might be feeling guilty for not spending quality time with their child.

How does this affect a child? It creates the conditional friendship. Friendships that are based only on benefits of the relationship, not the actual relationship. An overindulged child finds other kids useful, if and only if, the friends can give them things or status. Teasing of other children who do not have as much, or cutting off a friendship when the child no longer gets what he wants, and turning others against them, is common when child is in a conditional friendship.

COOL TO BE UNKIND

The need to be cool at all costs can mean do anything, including being cruel, to get a laugh out of other children. The bully who makes cracks at an overweight child, a special needs child, or a sensitive child, so that the other children, by-standers, get a laugh while poking fun at someone else. The laughter makes the bully feel even more empowered.

A parent of an overweight child shared a painful story with us. A group of boys called their daughter tubby, fatso, and a pig. When the boys ran out of names, they started a new tactic of being overly nice to her. One of the boys even asked her out on a date. The girl was so excited about the prospects of being cool and having a boyfriend, that she told her mother about the planned date. This mother was suspicious of the young man's motives and contacted the boy's parents. After a quick discussion with the boy's mother, she informed the girl's mother that it was all a misunderstanding. When the girl's mother told her daughter that it was a misunderstanding, the girl was embarrassed and did not want to go to school the following day. The girl went to school and was teased even more.

Children often learn this behavior of getting a laugh at someone else's expense from their parents. Adults joke about someone's large wife, make a quick comment about a feminine dad, or make mean remarks about other parent's intellectual capacity.

ACTS OF KINDNESS

In the day and age where coaches encourage their players to bully by trash talking, hurting children during games, and advocating cheating in sports, it is refreshing to see great sportsmanship. We were witness to an unconditional act of kindness recently by our sons' football coaches and were able to use it as a teachable moment for our children, as well as countless other children. A peewee football team from a neighboring town had not won a game all year and had not scored a single touchdown either. Our team was winning by a landslide. We saw our coaches happily discussing something; we assumed they were talking about the huge victory we were about to receive. We were so wrong; they were discussing how to allow the other team to score on us. When they did score it provided a lot of satisfaction to about 25 ten-year-olds, and about 50 of their siblings and parents. The children and parents were so happy they were in tears. Many of the parents went out of their way to thank us. The most heartwarming sight was watching two manly, forty-something-year-old coaches hug each other. What a wonderful lesson for the children and parents. It is cool to be kind!

LESSONS LEARNED

- Our children are going to be who they want to be.

- No parent can make up for their own past by overindulging a child.

- Be a role model for empathy and point out acts of kindness.

- We hope our next book will be called "Cool to be Kind" on all the unconditional and random acts of a child's kindness!

CHAPTER FOURTEEN
TEACHING CHILDREN HOW TO DO "THE RIGHT THING"

The world is a dangerous place, not because of those who do evil, but because those who look on and do nothing." Albert Einstein

BYSTANDER

Your child may not be bullied, but maybe is witnessing actions of bullying. He is the bystander of bullying. The bystander is the most influential person to the bully. He might not be doing the bullying themselves, but he may laugh when the bully makes fun of someone, or when the bully plays a trick on another child. A bystander's laugh alone adds fuel to the bully's fire. It is a clear sign to the bully, that the bullying is acceptable, maybe even enjoyed by others, and possibly, inspires the bully to continue the abusive behavior. The bystander usually means no harm, and although they do not take part in the actual bullying, they are inadvertently causing it to continue. Sometimes the bystanders are recruited to take part in the bullying activities.

A parent contacted us stating that her child was not bullied, but was witnessing her friends bully other children at school. Her child was somehow drawn to the bully like a moth to a flame. She did not want her child to be bullied or become a bully. The parent was not sure what to do. Her daughter talked openly about the bullying, and clearly knew it was wrong, yet did not know what to do to stop the friendship with the bully. Children definitely know who is doing the bullying, and who is bullied, in every school and neighborhood. They understand it is wrong, but do not know how to stop it without damaging their own reputation in the process.

The bystander actually holds all the power. In the instant of viewing the bullying, the bystander can be a leader. Bystanders have the ability to stop bullying in its tracks, if only they would take a stand and take action. The bystander has the power to dethrone the bully more than any teacher, parent, or law enforcement official. The bystander is the audience. Without an audience, the bully has no one to entertain or fuel his actions. Sometimes all it takes is for one child to say to the bully, "Knock it off. That's mean." The bully gets the message that bullying is un-cool. A kind word by the bystander to the victim could just save a child's life by knowing that there are other people out there who care.

Encourage the bystander to say something to the bully. If they are uncomfortable doing that, the child should consider saying something to the other bystanders. Suggest that they do not laugh with the bully, but show their disapproval through body language, such as a stern look or frown. A bystander could wait until others are not around and make it clear to the bully that their behavior is not acceptable and downright mean. Bystanders should let bullies know that they do not like or condone their behavior. A bystander could also talk to the principal informing them of the situation and ask that they remain, as the bystander, anonymous. They could do this in person, with a note, by telephone, or the Internet. Somehow, some way, it needs to be communicated to an adult in authority.

Bystanders often do not think independently and go with the flow. They need to be encouraged to think for themselves. Independent thinking is the driver for all success in all that we do as human beings. The bystander often does not want to get involved and say something to the bully for fear they may be bullied next. If the bystander truly understands the consequences of their inaction, perhaps they might do the right thing. Given the fact that the bystander already understands the consequences of bullying, evidenced by the fact they do not want to be bullied themselves, they should use this insight and stop bullying in its tracks.

Bystanders do not want to be isolated. They do not want to be made fun of, or laughed at for any reason. Ask the bystander how they would they feel if they were being bullied. Ask the bystander how they would feel if they did not say anything to anyone in authority, and then, tragically, the victim committed suicide. Ask them to imagine if it was their best friend, sister, brother, cousin that committed suicide over acts of bullying. Death is permanent, and a real possibility when it comes to extreme bullying. After the bystander thinks about this, they will clearly think twice before staying silent after witnessing bullying.

A high school coach told us a story of how a group of his very courageous players got together to inform him that his top player was both physically and emotionally abusing the less than stellar performers on the team. The discussion was kept confidential and the coach was going to look into the allegations. Instead of confronting his top player he decided to witness the abuse first hand. Most of the acts of bullying took place in the locker room after practice when the coaching staff was not present. When the coach walked into the locker room unannounced, he was sickened by what he witnessed. The coach did the right thing and removed his top player from the team. It was a very un-popular, yet courageous decision. The bystanders did the right thing, too, by speaking up, even if it meant losing the best player on team.

Do the Right Thing. Get Involved

You can encourage the bystander to do the right thing but if your child is a bystander, and is uncomfortable about saying something to the bully, the other bystanders or an adult at school, should accept his decision. There is no need to reprimand the bystander. You can lead by example. It is time for you as a parent, and a caring community member, to get involved.

Parents and Adults Need to Stop Being Passive Bystanders Too

We cannot tell you how many times parents have told us that they did not know how to intervene. When you see an incident of bullying, talk calmly to both parties and say something as simple as, "Gosh, I hope everybody here is being respectful to one another." It sounds old fashioned, but it really does work in that instant. Intervening is really easy to do. Find out as much detail as you can about the situation and contact the principal. You could even request that your inquiry remain anonymous, but stress that action needs to be taken as a child is in danger. If nothing is done, consider contacting the victim's family to make sure they are aware of the situation. Someone needs to take a stand and do the right thing, which is not necessarily the popular thing. Think about how you would feel if this was your child who was being abused or, God forbid, committed suicide over acts of bullying. If it were your child, you certainly would want someone to stand up and do the right thing. All parents and children should do the right thing.

Lessons Learned

- Empower the bystander.
- Do the right thing and get involved.
- Someone needs to take a stand and do the right thing, not necessarily the popular thing.

CHAPTER FIFTEEN
A SOCIAL MEDIA AND
ELECTRONIC BULLYING
DISCUSSION

We should start out and clearly state, we are fans. We support, and are fans of social media, including, Facebook and Twitter. We also believe children at the right age, and with the right amount of supervision, should have electronic devices or access to them. The key here is an understanding of your child's maturity level, and understanding that you, as the parent, must monitor and supervise these activities and devices. To be clear, we are not fans of those who *abuse* social media or electronic channels. Further, we also believe social media is not for everybody. We are not suggesting rules and laws, we are merely suggesting parents need to be informed and make decisions on an individualized basis.

With that disclaimer in place, let us talk a bit about how social media and all electronic channels can be a "bullying heaven" of sorts. Some children at 12 years of age are more mature than other children are. Some 12-year-old children are as mature as some 16 year olds are. Sometimes, 16-year-old children are at the same maturity level of most eleven year olds. You know where this is going. Judge your child's suitability for social media and electronic devices, such as cell phones, based on his ability to manage it, and concurrent to that, judge your own parental ability to monitor it regularly. Sometimes you can have a mature 12 year old who could probably manage a social media presence, but his parents simply do not have time to monitor it. This is dangerous. A parent should monitor a child's social media presence, regularly and thoroughly. Similarly, let us say if you have an immature 15 year old, with a parent who is willing to monitor the sites, social media is still not a good idea.

In the end, making the decision to allow your child to have social media or electronic online devices, must involve the parents' commitment to have access to, and to monitor his account regularly, as well as not being afraid to ask questions or intervene. Critical to the equation is that parents must be comfortable with their child's ability to manage and address uncomfortable, inappropriate, negative discussions on social media. The best rule to have is that your child must come to you if a discussion or situation arises in a social media forum that is uncomfortable for them. If you decide to proceed with allowing your child to have access to social media and electronic online devices, remember the minimum age for most social media sites is 13, and if your child joins when he is under 13, it is against the rules and possibly certain laws.

KEY RECOMMENDATIONS FOR PARENTS AND ALL ELECTRONIC MEDIA DEVICES

Admittedly, some of the following may feel as though it is too much, but we should all remember that we are both parent, and protector, of our children, and with that, we may not win any popularity contests. Remember, you are not going behind your child's back and spying. Spying is when you review their account without their knowledge. With our recommendations, everybody involved is aware, and it is out in the open. No spying, just protecting. Share with your child that your goal is to protect. Assure them it is not a trust issue with them; it is a trust question with most all strangers, and possibly some acquaintances. Be honest, confident, yet reassuring toward your child.

Consider implementing all of the below, based on your own family's situation when it comes to social media, electronic devices and usage.

1. Require access to the child's accounts to include email, Instant Messages (IMs), all sites, all phone and computer accounts.

2. Put parental controls software on the computer and make the child aware of the associated restrictions with that software.

3. Mandate there will not be any secret passwords.

4. Similarly, make your child understand that false or decoy accounts or pages, will not be tolerated.

5. Require that there is a clear understanding that what your child puts in writing or in photography online can never be erased and will live with him forever. It is a permanent record online, even if the information is erased from the hard drive. This has haunted many young people when it comes to new jobs, or relationships, as they get older. Give your child examples of how this could go dramatically awry for them.

6. Talk about the dangers attached to social media and electronic device activity, and prepare your child for bullying related events he may see or be subject to on any site.

7. Help your child understand the importance of kindness and good manners online.

8. Talk to your child about not letting his photo be taken by anyone he does not know.

9. Ask your child to report bullying online to the site management or parents if he witnesses bullying of any sort. Empower your child to be a good bystander.

10. Make an agreement with your child that he will not allow others to use his phone or electronic device without his full supervision.

11. Make certain your child promises to never, ever share passwords or account information with anyone other than you.

12. Develop criteria surrounding whom *to friend and not to friend* online.

13. All negative, even borderline, social media discussions should be avoided, and the content should be shared with parents immediately so that it can be discussed to determine if next steps are needed.

14. An agreement should be in place that states, as the parent, you will be monitoring the account regularly.

15. As parents, regularly review the account, emails, text and phone call history on your child's cell phone, as well as the social media friend list. If something feels intuitively wrong, it probably is.

16. Establish rules involving time spent on the computer, PDA's, phone, laptop, and anything that has a screen. Make sure your child is developing relationships with friends in person. Make sure your child socializes in person, not just online or via electronic media.

17. Do not let your child have a computer in his room. It simply prevents and solves many problems.

18. All phones and electronic devices should be shut down, and not be in your child's room, when they sleep. Do not let your child have their phone or an electronic device in the room during sleep hours or, they will not sleep. Period.

19. If any of the rules are broken, the account and electronic devices will be suspended. Period.

WHAT ARE THE SIGNALS MY CHILD IS CYBER-BULLIED?

While most of the signals that your child is bullied online are very similar to when your child is being bullied in person (see Chapter Three), there are some additional behaviors to watch for.

1. Your child spends long periods of time on social media, online, or on the phone texting.

2. Your child sees code words or language used by one or more children in any way on the account.

3. Your child seems to be upset, or withdrawn, directly after chatting online or texting.

4. Your child asks how to shut down an account.

5. Your child asks how to block friends and people from the account.

6. Your child shuts down the electronic device, laptop or phone whenever parents are nearby.

7. New phone numbers are showing up on your child's text and call history.

Types of Social Media and Electronic Bullying

- Name calling, direct or indirect.

- Discussion of your child by others using code language.

- Developing "I Hate XX" or "XX is a YY" groups, sites or pages.

- Gossiping.

- Sharing embarrassing stories, pictures or photos.

- Sexting: sexually harassing your child via text with pictures, photos, explicit language, texts filled with sexual innuendo, naked or suggestive pictures, and asking sexual questions in any way.

- Harassing with constant *forwards* text and emails that have inappropriate or embarrassing content.

- Harassing emails, texts or social media communications asking your child embarrassing or humiliating questions.

- High frequency of emails, texts, social media messages or instant messages in rapid succession that make your child uncomfortable.

- Developing false accounts in your child's name and communicating online using his name or account.

- Falsely portraying or imitating your child online in anyway.

- Development of any site, page or any online presence using your child's image, name or personal information in any negative way or without your child's permission.

How Does a Parent Stop Online or Electronic Bullying?

- Stay calm and focused.

- Give your child suggestions on how to stop it himself. Use judgment here. If it is serious, you should intervene immediately and remove your child from the issue, but sometimes your child should be empowered to do so first.

- Review all inappropriate content, print a copy, or save to the hard drive.

- Document everything.

- Regardless of the medium, social media, texting, IM, or email, log on and write a note to all offenders identifying yourself as your child's parent. Ask them to cease, and inform them if they do not, then their parents will be told. Require apologies from all. If your child was involved, make certain he apologizes for his part.

- If it stops and starts again in the same or other ways, contact the parents. Review Chapters Four and Six.

- Keep copies of all communications.

- If it is serious, contact an attorney for counsel.

- Make certain the bully's parents see the offensive online communications so they clearly understand the problem.

- Remember to require that all communications regarding your child by the cyber bullies should cease. You cannot be thorough enough. All gossiping, discussion, and secrets should stop immediately. A written agreement is advisable in this situation. See Chapter Seventeen for a template to use.

- Shut down all social media and email accounts until the issue has passed. If your child wants to have those activities reinstated later, simply start new accounts under a new name.

- Report the bullies to the social media site or online source that was involved.

- Monitor and search sites for several weeks to ascertain the issue has passed.

- If anything reoccurs, contact the cyber-bullying police unit and share all the documentation. Make sure they contact the offenders directly. Ask the officer for confirmation of contact and a report.

- Do your homework and review your state's law regarding cyber-bullying.

- Encourage your child to stay away from electronic media until he feels safe and comfortable.

- Keep talking and stay informed regarding how your child feels about all of the events.

- Consider going to your county building and getting an order of protection for your child. The county staff will help you execute this swiftly.

The key again is to stop it early and comprehensively. If you do not stop this activity as soon as you see it, it grows.

LESSONS LEARNED

- Think twice and consider this chapter before allowing your child to have an electronic online device or a social media account.

- Be honest and open with your child. Let him know you trust him, but the rest of the online world is a question mark.

- Be clear about the fact you will be monitoring his online and electronic media activity.

- Be vigilant about spot-checking and thoroughly checking the membership of all social media and electronic devices your child owns.

- If bullying occurs, stay calm, be an adult and intervene.

- Stop bullying early and comprehensively.

CHAPTER SIXTEEN
WHAT VICTIMS AND PARENTS OF VICTIMS CAN DO TO PROTECT THEMSELVES

START EARLY

As we have stressed, the most important thing to do when your child is bullied is report the situation quickly to the school. Discussions regarding bullying should start early in your child's life. Research has shown that bullying starts as early as preschool, and in some cases continues throughout elementary school and beyond. When your child starts preschool, or kindergarten, discuss with him in simple terms the meaning of bullying, and handling a situation if it occurs. Role-play with your child on how to say no, and stop, to another child if he is mean.

Give your child simple examples of the ways children are bullied in school:

- Being hit or kicked by another child
- Repeatedly being called names
- Purposely excluding a child from games and other activities

Discuss with your child what he should do if he is bullied. He should firmly tell the child, or children, to stop. Your child needs to inform a teacher and needs to tell you, the parent, about every situation that makes him feel uncomfortable. A child needs to feel he has control over situations that happen in life; children learn to be helpless, or they learn how to manage situations, at an early age. The ability to feel empowered at a young age is a skill that will not only help at age six, but also at 46.

Discuss with your daycare provider, preschool and kindergarten teachers how they handle situations of bullying. Find out this information *before* you need it. If you do have a situation where you need to contact the teacher, make sure that the teacher does not solve the problem by bringing the two children in the room together. What the teacher will do is ask the bullied child to rehash the incident and ask how he feels. This technique of conflict resolution has been the gold standard in education. It is wrong, and does not work. It actually makes the situation worse by embarrassing or humiliating the victim a second time, in addition to making the victim feel he is in trouble. Even at a young age, the mini bully feels powerful and may use the comments made during the intervention session against the victim in the future. Teachers often underestimate the mini bully's ability to manipulate the situation by lying and twisting the truth. The bully might be forced to give a fake apology that seems sincere to the adult involved. The mini bully might be accustomed to playing sweet and innocent at home to get out of trouble. Insist that the mini bully have a conversation with the adult in charge alone, and that the adult does not use the victim's name. The teacher, or another adult, could say, "It has come to our attention that you have been treating some children badly, by calling them mean names and not allowing them to play games. We do not allow this at our school, and it must stop. I am going to discuss this with your parents. There will be a consequence for this behavior."

Keeping the victim's name out of the discussion, will focus the attention on the bully's behavior. Hopefully, the teacher will have a consequence for the mini bully, such as missing a favorite school activity.

It is important that the school and the teachers are accountable. Ask the teacher what will happen next. Will the bully's parents be notified? Will this be reported to the principal? Find out what will happen, when it will happen, when the teacher will follow up with you on action steps, and what the teacher will do to keep an eye on any future incidents of bullying. Be sure to follow up to confirm action was taken. This may sound extreme for bullying at a young age, but most parents we have talked to wish they had stepped in earlier to protect their child.

We did not think to talk to our children about bullying when they were six years old, but we can help other parents of small children. Parents should have a discussion with their children regarding bullying as early as kindergarten. This action could help protect their child in the future.

BE SEEN AND HEARD

Be seen and be heard to protect your child. It is a common theme among parents of victims that they do not want to talk to anyone about their bullied child for fear that their child will be viewed as an outcast. Just like the child being bullied, the parent of a bullied child can often feel isolated. It is important that the dirty details of your child's situation are not shared, but it needs to be known that the parents of the bullied child are not going to stand for these repeated disrespectful acts of abuse against their child. It is important to be professional and respectful when talking to the school and other parents, including the parents of the bully.

Before participating in any discussions regarding bullying, take a deep breath before you speak. Listen to what the other person is saying, try not to interrupt, and wait for them to finish their thoughts. Keep in mind they may not use the same courteous listening techniques that you will use, but demonstrate your professionalism while still stating your point.

People discussing bullying will often say things such as *kids will be kids*, tell your child to *toughen up*, this has *been going on for centuries* or *it will pass*. Practice your response for these comments because you will hear the same things repeatedly. The comment we hear most often is that *we were bullied as kids and we turned out just fine*. I always say, "Things are different now from when we were children." Further, bullying is not normal behavior and there is absolutely no reason to have to endure it. With the increase in technology used by kids, the role models of mean people being glamorized in the media, plus the lack of adult supervision, has made being a kid and avoiding bullying much more difficult these days. Be clear that it is not just "kids being kids." The bully is disrespectful and is mean and it needs to stop.

Be seen, and be proud to participate, at school and social events. If your child is bullied, it is important to be involved and volunteer for school activities. You are then able to keep an eye on day-to-day activities, and make your presence known. Volunteer for any activity in which your child is interacting with other children, such as school parties, dances and sporting activities. This does not mean your child needs to be glued to you. Your child should do what they would normally do, as if you were not there. After the event, ask your child if he had fun at the event, why or why not, and if he felt comfortable with your presence. At adult social events, well-meaning parents often would speak to us with pity in their voice, in hushed tones, asking about how things were going with our child. Some parents were genuinely concerned, which we appreciated. Others were just looking for a piece of juicy gossip and could not wait to get home to call the rest of their friends to tell them that we looked horrible and were depressed. In both cases, we proudly said, without getting into detail, that we were doing quite well, and we were not going to stand for this kind of disrespect to our children, or any child for that matter. Equally critical on these occasions, it was imperative to be positive and happy. In our cases, we were being authentic because solutions we developed for our children had begun to work. However, there were times when we did not feel like smiling and chatting, but we tried. It is important to articulate how strong and terrific your child is, and how proud you are of your child. Be a role model by being seen and being heard. You will not be stepped on, act like a victim, or be disrespected. Yes, other parents will talk about you and make some positive, and some negative, comments. Stay strong. Be brave. Be seen and be heard. Do not let anybody get you down.

LESSONS LEARNED

- Start early to discuss bullying with your children.
- Practice with them how to say no to bullying.
- Be seen and heard.
- Delay the flood of technology in your children's life.
- Limit their time using technology.

CHAPTER SEVENTEEN
HOW DO I HELP MY SCHOOL
AND COMMUNITY DEVELOP AN
ANTI-BULLYING PROGRAM?

It should be clear that navigating schools and communities as you deal with bully ing could be challenging and frustrating. Our experience with our own school district is probably typical. The district, superintendent, school board and princi-pals start out in disbelief or denial of the issue. From there, they slowly realize the gravity of the issue, and then typically need to assign a task force.

This sounds a bit frustrating, but it is worth it if you want to solve your community's bullying issue.

Please remember the good news is:

- Doing *something* is always better than doing nothing.

- You *can* get past this issue. Many formerly bullied children are living successful lives to prove that life goes on.

- You can get back to happiness. We did.

- There is no better feeling than knowing you are doing the right thing, especially when others put up roadblocks in your way. Determination is empowering.

- Solving a bullying problem in your school or community does *save lives!*

- Let us say that again. *You are saving lives*!

That is the good news. There is no bad news, but there are realities to be aware of when starting an anti-bullying program. Whether you are in the thick of solving your own child's bullying issue, or you are building a new program, there are challenges that will confront you. Do not let these minor issues deter you. Stay focused and do not lose faith. Email us and will give you a pep talk. You can visit us at solutionsforbullying.com.

Communities are fascinating to observe. There are so many layers and complexities. Additionally, communities tend to have personalities. As a nation, we tend to have great patriotism and a strong sense of pride. These sentiments trickle down to the community level in most cases. Communities want to believe they are close to being Mayberry or Main Street USA. While generally positive, this turns negative when a community member, or group of members, identifies that *Mayberry may not be so Mayberry-ish*. In many cases, most community members take any criticism, even well stated, constructive criticism, personally. Further, when one group identifies an issue, there tends to be divisions and sides taken. When we found out that the bullying issue in our schools was severe and we started to talk about it openly, people reacted in one of three ways:

1. They were concerned and wanted to learn more

2. They feigned concern and put their heads in the sand

3. They did not react, but behind our backs, told everyone they knew that we were exaggerating and there really was not a problem.

It is important that you treat all three groups with great respect. Stay on task, stay focused, and know you are doing the right thing.

GETTING STARTED

There are many ways to skin a cat as they say, but we will share our recommendations based on our experience and research. Our experience with our own community was challenging, but successful. We knew little about the topic of bullying, and had very little idea about an approach. The following is based on what we learned.

First, a summary of what happened when we decided to take action. Our children were bullied. During the period in which we were solving the issue, we built a committee of parents and experts. From the committee we developed a larger-scale task force was developed by the district, and many of the original recommendations from our homegrown committee were reviewed and implemented five months after the original presentation. Many of our recommendations are to be phased in over two years. This is warp-speed for schools. It sounds like a long time, but there was a summer in that time span. Be prepared, most schools will move at this speed or slower. If you are patient with your schools, superintendent and school board, amazing things can happen. Remember: you may not be able to do all of this, so select what works for you. One of my favorite lyrics by Steve Winwood proudly believes you "can make the sun shine from pure desire."

START TALKING OPENLY ABOUT YOUR CHILD'S ISSUE

While my family was trudging through the very thick of it, I told virtually no one about our trials with the bullies. Close family and people in the community that learned of the situation would ask how things were going in very hushed tones. People were genuinely concerned, and I still appreciate their concern.

What I finally learned about one year into the bullying situation is that people thought I was embarrassed about this issue. I never was embarrassed. I kept quiet because I found that many parents in my generation have absolutely no filter when it comes to sharing information with their own children. Over the course of several years, if I chatted with some parents about a challenge one of my sons was having, some parents would immediately share that information with their children. In turn, my children would be teased.

My hair still stands on end when I remember a specific episode where my husband and I had to be very clear, if not stern, with a family about next steps we would take if their child did not stop gossiping and taunting my son. I remember the mother looked at me and said, "Well, we don't want anybody to be embarrassed. Our goal is to prevent your son from being known as the bullied child and to prevent our son from being known as the bully." News flash: the bully should be embarrassed that he did something wrong and my son did not. My reply to that mother was that I was not embarrassed, but I did understand how her family would feel embarrassed and ashamed. The lesson here is do not be embarrassed. Talk about the issue, so that it can be resolved.

Once my family decided to put a successful solution in place, I opened up, shared the fact that, yes, my son is bullied, and yes, I understand there is a large problem in our schools. My co-author did the same. Within two weeks of getting the word out, we both started getting phone calls from mother after mother sharing horror stories about the bullying their child was enduring. I finished every phone call the same way, "Do not be embarrassed or ashamed. The bullies and their families should feel ashamed, not you. Bullies are exhibiting abnormal behavior. Your child is not acting abnormally. Your child is not inviting bullying or asking for it. Your child is simply being who he is. Remember that. Hang in there, and please know, we are going to get this fixed in our community, I promise you."

START DIAGNOSING YOUR COMMUNITY

Once you start opening up, keep track of the numbers of incidents you are told about and who is involved, but keep confidences if families ask for anonymity. Get a feel for the groups of children and the types of bullying that is going on. Ask your children, your children's friends, or older kids who have gone through the same school about the incidents. Talk to teachers. Talk to the school counselor. Talk to camp counselors in your park district or youth group leaders at your church. These leaders hear many stories from children about school social environments. Be an investigative reporter. Typically when you know of a few cases, there are more. It may not be a huge problem in your community, but it is good to catch it in its early stages if it is growing.

RESEARCH BULLYING

We gave you a series of statistics and some background on the topic of bullying in Chapter Two, but learn more yourself. All you have to do is Google the term bullying, and you will find information. Your state will have specific materials that will be helpful in school discussions. Assemble a short presentation from this information and have it ready once you are poised to approach the school.

BUILD A MULTI-TALENTED GROUP OF CONCERNED COMMUNITY MEMBERS

If you can gather five to ten families who will support you and attend a school board meeting, this is a good start. Try to find parents and community leaders who are profes-sionals such as attorneys, school board members, social workers, local bullying experts, local law enforcement, park district leaders, faith leaders, adolescent psychologists, media reporters, and teachers. Try to have equal representation from each of the schools in your district on your committee. This is not critical, but it is helpful. Gather perspectives from everyone, and incorporate the information into a general committee presentation. You may decide after your committee meets that another member may be better suited as the leader or you may want to have a co-chair.

CALL OR EMAIL THE SUPERINTENDENT AND PRESIDENT
OF THE SCHOOL BOARD

This is when it starts to get spicy. Superintendents are always overworked and gen-erally overstretched. School boards are alternately very engaged, or can be disengaged. Play it safe, and make the email contact positive and ask if you can arrange a meeting between both of them with your committee. Explain in a positive manner that the committee would like to discuss how to leverage the existing anti-bullying policies and procedures—even if you believe there are none, compromise and give them a sense of collaboration—and work together to make the policies stronger. Share in a positive way that you are aware of a growing concern involving bullying among parents in the district. Try your best not to appear accusatory in any way. Recognize that they are busy, as are their staff and teachers, and you are there to help them with solutions. Be extremely polite, but be a polite nuisance. Ask for the meeting to take place in the next two to three weeks.

It is important to remember that the superintendent and the school board may genu-inely believe their current policy is effective, or as many schools say, their *zero-tolerance* is quite effective. Typically, they are unaware of the level and seriousness of the bullying issue. Try to have patience, as these individuals learn more on the issue. The situation is fresh, well understood and raw to you, but it is new and not understood at all, to them. Once you have the meeting scheduled, meet with your co-chair and team to strategize how to best get the superintendent and school board up to speed on the issue of bullying;

get them motivated to change the status quo; and, help them feel like everybody is on the same team.

MEET WITH YOUR COMMITTEE TO REVIEW THE PRESENTATION AND STRATEGIZE

Meet with your committee and determine how you can accomplish key things in that first meeting with the school board and superintendent. Key points include:

 a. Getting their attention and making them realize quickly there is a valid and sizeable problem in your school system.

 b. Making them feel like you are there to partner with them, and that your team is willing to work on the solution actively, not just make recommendations.

 c. Providing short-term and longer-term solutions that can be implemented in phases.

 d. Helping them understand that your team empathizes with their workload, understands the parental politics involved, and that you know the solutions are challenging, but the team believes solutions can be achieved.

REVIEW THE PREVENTIVE POLICIES, PROTOCOL AND TACTICS CURRENTLY IN PLACE

Most schools claim they have a zero-tolerance policy. Typically, zero-tolerance has zero meaning. In this situation, there is no policy, or procedure, it is simply a sentence in the school handbook. However, some schools do have some protocol in place. Use them and build on them.

DEVELOPING PROGRAM CRITERIA, POLICY, PROTOCOL AND TACTICAL IDEAS FOR YOUR DISTRICT TO CONSIDER IMPLEMENTING

Before starting to develop an anti-bullying program policy, protocol and tactics, it is helpful as a team, to develop criteria for your program and its components. Here is a general criteria starter list:

The District Anti-bullying program:

- Should be practical, easy to implement with clear instructions
- Have a clear definition of bullying

- The program will include:
    - o A clear, and stated, process for investigating bullying incidents
    - o A tracking and reporting system for incidents
    - o Forms to track the bully and insert in his file
    - o Surveys in the beginning and end of each year
    - o Staff training on definition, prevention and how to intervene in bullying incidents
    - o A prevention program
    - o Bystander training
    - o Victim reporting systems
    - o Bully reform and consequences protocol

ANTI-BULLYING PROGRAM PHASES

Chapter Two discussed the bully cycle. There are three phases:

- Prevention
- Victim reporting and victim support
- Consequences and reform measures for the bully

The following anti-bullying program ideas are organized among those three parts of the bully cycle, and can serve as thought starters for your team. As you will learn, there are hundreds of good ideas out there and each school should tailor the ideas to their own needs. Many of these ideas are complimentary and are a starting point for all new programs.

PREVENTION

Ideally, if more schools put a stronger emphasis on empathy with a strong message of acceptance of all students, and schools embedded these messages into the curriculum, many of the following tactics would not be necessary. However, few parents and schools emphasize empathy and acceptance of all.

Do not send out *good behavior contracts* or *conduct promises* to all students at the beginning. They do not work, do not mean anything, and dilutes your message.

Consider the following anti-bullying components and concepts:

- Use pre-packaged character building systems such as PBIS and other well-referenced school programs that help model behavior

- Embed social and emotional learning (SEL) concepts into the curriculum at schools. See Collaborative for Academic, Social and Emotional Learning at www.casel.org for information.

- Encourage adult supervision in all open areas in schools. You need to have teachers and staff *actively watching for bullying in hallways, locker rooms, lunchrooms, bathrooms, buses, and gyms.* These are areas where most bullying is executed, without notice. *Staff should learn behaviors to observe, and they should learn how to intervene in situations.* This is critical.

- Organize parental assemblies where experts talk about bullying and how parents can prevent, manage and stop bullying in their own community.

- Organize an internally developed assembly where key speakers discuss bullying from various perspectives. There is a complimentary "Anti-bullying School Assembly" script on our site, solutionsforbullying.com. Potential content for the school's assembly includes:

  o An introduction to new anti-bullying policies and procedures:

    ■ This is an opportunity for the superintendent and principal to let all students know *there is a new sheriff in town* and that the sheriff sees all bullying, and deals with bullying very directly, and is determined to stop it.

  o A police officer discussing the charges that can be made against a bully as young as nine years of age

  o An adult victim of bullying telling his story

  o A parent who has lost their child to suicide as a result of bullying

  o A young adult who was formerly a bully and reformed himself

  o A formerly incarcerated young adult who started his criminal career as a bully

  o A social worker or psychologist

  o An attorney to talk about civil lawsuits

- Teacher and staff development:

  o Training on bullying

  o Definition and identification

  o Inform staff that ignoring only makes it worse, and telling a child to ignore it fuels the bully's will to continue bullying

  o Intervention skills and tools

  o Promoting respect

- Bystander Training: Train children to be independent thinkers and speak out on behalf of victims. There should be a student group involved with this effort to ensure peer-to-peer support.

- Mix-it-up Day: Children are asked one day each month to sit with children other than their friends at lunch or in free time

- Lunch and Learns: Lunch periods devoted to peer-to-peer discussions, where older, very popular high school children speak about topics such as *bullying is lame and un-cool*.

- Citizenship and leadership programs to teach children how to be a good school citizen

VICTIM REPORTING AND VICTIM SUPPORT

Reporting:

- Anonymous reporting box placed in school hallways

- Report forms available on the school web site to be submitted by students, parents or staff online

- Email and texting reporting tools. There are several, well-known online reporting tools and systems designed specifically for schools. There are others as well.

- Student passes available to allow students to speak to guidance counselors during the school day when needed, without question

- A 1-800 # for reporting

- A parental help hotline

- A reporting tool resource directory on the school web site that includes the local cyber-bulling police information, attorneys, and social workers and therapists

- A district-wide ombudsman to arbitrate bullying situations among families

Victim Support:

- Guidance Counselors specifically trained on bullying support are important to success. Currently most guidance counselors do not know how to guide victims of bullying properly, and to help the child with key strategies

- Therapy available through free community centers or YMCAs

- Lists of specialized therapists who really understand bullying, social skills, and anxiety in their communities

- Deliver *red-alerts* on known bullies to all teachers and staff to monitor the bully, and be sensitive to and watchful of the victim.

CONSEQUENCES AND REFORM MEASURES FOR THE BULLY

- *Do not use* peer-to-peer conflict resolution. It re-victimizes the victim by making them live through the bullying again with the bully. The bully learns nothing, laughs about it later, and the victim becomes more scared.

- Punishments such as *detentions and suspensions* do not work. They only serve to *kick up the hornet's nest* and make the bully more angry and vengeful. Do not punish. Instead, provide clear consequences that drive the bully to reflect, introspect, understand and grow. Recommended consequences for the bully:

  o Make sure everything that is said to a bully is delivered clearly with a firm voice. Put everything in writing and in his file.

  o Share with the offender there are criminal laws that may have broken. Possible charges that can be pressed, depending on your state's laws, include:

    ■ Harassment

    ■ Hate crimes

    ■ Stalking

    ■ Assault and battery

    ■ And, many other charges

  o Share the possible types of civil suits that can be directed to the bully child's family if the victim's family pursues more significant action and the bully does not cease their behavior.

  o Require the bully to share every single name of anyone who is participating in bullying the victim, and then talk to each of the offenders along with providing consequences.

  o Require the bully to do a full research report on bullying that clearly helps him understand how their actions affect both the victim and himself.

    ■ The report can be written during lunch and during before-school detentions where someone is supervising

107

- ■ The report is presented orally to a volunteer panel and graded
- ○ Require the bully to write separate apologies to the victim, the school, his own family, as well as the victim's family, articulating how his actions are wrong, why they are wrong, and how he will act differently moving forward
- ○ Require the bully to perform community and volunteer service in the area for two to twenty hours over one to two months
- ○ Produce a video on this topic designed for the bully to better understand the impact of bullying on both the victim and himself. If you need a starting point, take a peek at the complimentary video script outline on our web site at www.solutionsforbullying.com
  - ○ Using a facilitation guide, assign a trained guidance counselor, or principal, to discuss the impact the bullying has on the victim, on the bully himself, and on the school environment as well as the learnings from the video with the bully.
  - ○ From the above discussion, have the bully write out what he has learned, and how he will be operating differently as a result of these findings.
  - ○ If it has become clear that the bully is not likely to completely stop and change his ways, use the template family contract included, and develop an agreement signed by the bully family and victim family that states:
    - ■ The bully will cease and desist all bullying behavior
    - ■ The bully will not talk about the victim in any way for any reason
    - ■ The bully will never discuss the incidents, the contract, or any information regarding the victim
    - ■ The bully will not speak in code or in any medium in any way regarding the victim
    - ■ The bully will keep some distance between the victim and himself physically
  - ○ In more serious cases, arrange a conversation with a police officer to make it clear to the bully what the next steps will be if he continues the behavior.

KEY OBJECTIONS YOU WILL HEAR FROM THE SCHOOL DISTRICT WHEN DEVELOPING AN ANTI-BULLYING SYSTEM

1. The district simply does not have the time or money.
   Response: We understand and that is why we are glad to do all the work and raise the money needed.

2. Is the problem that bad?
   Response: Yes, it is pervasive and here are our numbers to prove it. If you would feel more comfortable hearing from all of the families affected, we can have them contact you directly or come to several board meetings.

3. We need to form a task force.
   Response: Great. May one of our team members be a leader on it? When do we get started and how can I help?

4. We already have a policy in place.
   Response: Yes, we understand that was a workable policy when it was developed, but it clearly needs enhancement based on the rising volume and severity of incidents.

5. You must understand that while you feel the bullies are not being addressed, we get just as many calls about how harshly the bullies have been dealt with in the past. We can never make everybody happy.
   Response: Yes, we understand all parents want to be advocates for their children, but in the case of the bullies, they need to be stopped and the administration cannot allow themselves to be bullied. We are here to support you even when parents bully you. By the way, this is not about making everybody happy, this is about protecting children and providing a safe, comfortable learning environment.

SAMPLE TOOLS AND RESOURCES

A. Bullies 101 Facilitator's Guide

Designed to use in tandem with the Bullies 101 film or can be adapted for use without the film. The Bullies 101 Script Outline is available at www.solutionsforbullying.com.

Introduction:

Bullies 101 is an educational video tool designed to be used as part of a larger anti-bulling program within the school system to:

1. Help teachers, staff, administrators and adults acclimate to the issue and better understand the effects of bullying as well as recommended approaches.

2. Help children who are currently bullying to understand the negative impact of bullying on a victim as well as the negative impact bullying has on a bully.

Bullies 101 will assist teachers, staff and students in understanding the definition of bullying with real examples and clear explanations. It will also drive reflection, introspection and hopefully prevent bullying acts. Similarly, it will aid in the reform process for current bullies.

There are three separate components to Bullies 101:

A. An **Educational Training Overview** for teachers, staff, administrators and parents created to inform, define and manage the challenging issue of bullying in our schools today. Most importantly, it stresses the need to intervene.

B. A set of eight **Interactive Student Modules** produced to use with students who have bullied as a part of their consequences. Staff will be able to choose which modules to use based on that specific student's needs. The eight modules are:

1. The definition of bullying

2. An interview with a victim of constant harassment

3. An overview and definition of cyber-bullying

4. An interview with a victim who became a bully

5. An interview with a victim of cyber-bullying

6. An interview with an adult who still feels the pain and effects of name-calling, and worse, from her childhood

7. An interview with a victim of physical bullying

8. A clearly stated definition of possible criminal and legal consequences of bullying

C. **A Facilitator's Guide To the Student Modules** is provided to assist a social worker, counselor, or teacher in the *teachable moment* discussion with a student immediately after viewing each module.

Important to note: Each child selected to view one or more modules should see both The Definition of Bullying module, and The Explanation of Criminal Charges and Consequences module as a part of every session, in addition to any other pertinent modules.

POTENTIAL USES FOR BOTH VERSIONS WITHIN THE BULLIES 101 TOOL

Bullies 101: Educational Overview

- **Teacher Training Sessions:** The video can be shared with all staff to help understand what bullying is *and the importance of intervening.*

- **Parent Training or Series of Lectures:** Can be used among parents of bullies and within a larger training and enlightenment series

- **During Student Assemblies:** Can be used as an educational tool with children during a school event to help them understand what bullying is and its impact on all involved.

Bullies 101 – Student Modules

- **After the First Strike:** Select the video module appropriate for the specific child's situation. Use the accompanying questions and guidance commentary that is provided in the Facilitator's Guide with a child found to be bullying after his first incident. The Guide will support an appropriate discussion and promote the child to self-introspect and to reflect on his actions to affect his behavior.

- **At Assemblies:** During the first week of school, or anytime for that matter, present the videos during an assembly along with key speakers, such as a member of law enforcement, former bullies, former victims, and possibly experts to help all students understand the serious dangers and negative impact of bullying

FACILITATOR'S GUIDE FOR INTERACTIVE STUDENT MODULES

The concept is for the school staff and adult such as the social worker, counselor, or teacher designated to present the video in a teachable moment-fashion, to present the video modules based on the students learning needs, pausing at key points to have a discussion, ask questions, and interact.

The goal is to drive introspection, reflection, and hopefully attitudinal change.

The Teachable Moment Process: Facilitator's Guide for All Modules

Module #1: The Definition of Bullying. This should be played *every time* a child is identified as bullying, along with other modules that are pertinent to each situation.

Pause : Questions

- How do all of those statements make you feel?

- Do you understand what coercion is?

- Do you understand what recruiting other bullies means?

- Have you done any of those things mentioned?

- Do you think you have been bullying based on these definitions?

- Can you give me an example of one of your bullying behaviors?

- What is the difference between teasing or joking and bullying? **Answer:** teasing or joking becomes bullying when, 1) The victim of the joke reacts badly or sadly, 2) The victim asks the person joking to stop, or 3) The victim of the joke is not allowed to reciprocate the joke and is demeaned as a result of that situation. Provide an example such as Joey jokes *you walk funny and you look like an ape* to Tom. Tom becomes embarrassed and says nothing. Joey continues and starts making ape-like sounds around him.

- Why do you think you bullied another child?

- How did it make you feel?

- How do you think it made your victim feel?

- At then end of our session, we will be viewing a video that helps students understand what criminal and legal consequences you may face if you continue to bully.

Module #2: Victim Turned Bully

Pause : Questions

- Do you understand you can stop the cycle? Just because someone bullies you, or someone around you bullied someone else, does not mean it is acceptable. Tell me why this child started bullying?

- Were you ever bullied?

- Tell me about that time?

- How did it make you feel?

- Why did you then decide it was a good idea to bully?

- Tell me about how you bullied and give examples.

- How does that make you feel to have the label of a bully?

- How do you feel about the fact that you made someone feel sad, inadequate, and alone?

- Why did you choose that person to bully?

- How would you feel if this happened to you?

- How do you think the victim felt about what you said or did?

- Are you going to stop bullying?

- What are you going to do to make up for your behavior?

- What is the difference between teasing, joking and bullying? **Answer:** teasing and joking becomes bullying when, 1) The victim of the joke reacts badly or sadly, 2) The victim asks the person joking to stop, or 3) The victim of the joke is not allowed to reciprocate the joke and is demeaned as a result of that situation. Provide an example such as Joey jokes that *you walk funny and you look like an ape* to Tom. Tom becomes embarrassed and says nothing. Joey continues and starts making ape-like sounds around him.

- Tell me what you can do to stop bullying people and to help stop other bullies?

- Are you going to intervene if you see bullying, or tell an adult?

- Did you know that the number one reason children nine to fifteen years of age commit suicide is because they have been bullied and cannot take it anymore?

- Why should you do this?

- At then end of our session, we will be viewing a video that helps students understand what criminal and legal consequences you may face if you continue to bully.

Module # 3: The Definition of Cyber-Bullying

Pause: Questions

- Have you been doing any of these things?

- Please share examples of these actions, and share what you, specifically did.

- Can you give a definition and examples of other cyber-bullying?

- Why do you think this is hurtful?

- How do you think your victim felt when they read, saw, or learned about your cyber-bullying?

- How would you feel if this happened to you?

- What do you think will happen to your victim's reputation and social life as a result of your actions?

- What is the difference between teasing, joking and bullying? **Answer:** teasing and joking becomes bullying when, 1) The victim of the joke reacts badly or sadly, 2) The victim asks the person joking to stop, or 3) The victim of the joke is not allowed to reciprocate the joke and is demeaned as a result of that situation. Provide an example such as Joey jokes *you walk funny and you look like an ape* to Tom. Tom becomes embarrassed and says nothing. Joey continues and starts making ape-like sounds around him. The same is true online. When a victim of a joke is not allowed to have equal time to joke back, or is demeaned in any way, it is bullying.

- Are you going to stop bullying?

- What is your plan to make up for your behavior?

- At then end of our session, we will be viewing a video that helps students understand what criminal and legal consequences you may face if you continue to bully.

Module #4: Victim of Cyber-Bullying

Pause : Questions

- Did you think what happened to student(s) was just a joke or just joking around? Do you see now that it is not just joking around?

- Would you like this to happen to you?

- How would you feel if this happened to you?

- Tell me what you can do to stop bullying people and to help stop other bullies?

- Why should you do this?

- What is the difference between teasing, joking and bullying? **Answer:** teasing and joking becomes bullying when, 1) The victim of the joke reacts badly or sadly, 2) The victim asks the person joking to stop, or 3) The victim of the joke is not allowed to reciprocate the joke and is demeaned as a result of that situation. Provide an example such as Joey jokes *you walk funny and you look like an ape* to Tom. Tom becomes embarrassed and says nothing. Joey continues and starts making ape-like sounds around him. Same is true online. When a victim of a joke is not allowed to have equal time to joke back or is demeaned in any way, it is bullying.)

- Do you understand that you can be reported to the police for either in-person bullying or cyber-bullying? The police will visit your home and you can be charged with a crime.

- Are you going to stop the bullying? How will you make up for the hurt you caused?

- At then end of our session, we will be viewing a video that helps students understand what criminal and legal consequences you may face if you continue to bully.

Module #5: Former Victim of Severe Name-Calling and Bullying

Pause: Questions

- Do you understand why that woman was made to feel, in her words, worthless when she was bullied as a young girl? Do you know why that is wrong?

- What if someone made you feel badly about your physical appearance or a personality trait? How would you feel?

- Do you understand that this adult woman *still* feels badly about how she was treated when she was in elementary, middle school and high school?

- Do you want to be responsible for making someone feel that badly?

- What can you do to solve this problem?

- What can you do when you see someone bullying?

- When you see someone be mean, or when you see a student ignored or excluded, what can you do?

- What is the difference between teasing, joking and bullying? **Answer:** teasing/joking becomes bullying when, 1) The victim of the joke reacts badly or sadly, 2) The victim asks the person joking to stop, or 3)

The victim of the joke is not allowed to reciprocate the joke and is demeaned as a result of that situation. Provide an example such as Joey jokes *you walk funny and you look like an ape* to Tom. Tom becomes embarrassed and says nothing. Joey continues and starts making ape-like sounds around him. Same is true online. When a victim of a joke is not allowed to have equal time to joke back or is demeaned in any way, it is bullying.

- Did you know that the number one reason children nine to 15 years of age commit suicide is because they have been bullied and cannot take it anymore?

- Do you understand that you can be reported to the police for either in-person bullying or cyber-bullying? The police will visit your home and you can be charged with a crime.

- At then end of our session, we will be viewing a video that helps students understand what criminal and legal consequences you may face if you continue to bully.

- Are you going to stop bullying?

- Are you going to intervene when you see bullying?

- How are you going to make up for the hurt you caused?

Module #6: Victim of Physical Bullying

Pause: Questions

- Do you understand that verbal bullying can lead to physical bullying?

- Taunting can escalate quickly. Do you see how?

- Tell me how you physically bullied this child?

- Why?

- Do you understand that your anger is wrong and misplaced?

- This is not healthy behavior. It damages you and the victim. Can you tell me why?

- Do you understand how being disrespectful can lead to very serious damage?

- This girl was in the hospital for three weeks because her bully started out with teasing and over a few months started physically hurting her. How would you feel if that was you?

- Did you know that the number one reason children nine to fifteen years of age commit suicide is because they have been bullied and cannot take it anymore?

- Can you imagine if one of your friends, sister, or brother, committed suicide? How would you feel about the bully who caused them to go to that length to escape the bullying?

- How would you feel in general if this happened in your school?

- What is the difference between teasing and joking and bullying? **Answer:** teasing and joking becomes bullying when, 1) The victim of the joke reacts badly or sadly, 2) The victim asks the person joking to stop, or 3) The victim of the joke is not allowed to reciprocate the joke and is demeaned as a result of that situation. Provide an example such as Joey jokes *you walk funny and you look like an ape* to Tom. Tom becomes embarrassed and says nothing. Joey continues and starts making ape-like sounds around him. Same is true online when a victim of a joke is not allowed to have equal time to joke back or is demeaned in any way, it is bullying.

- At then end of our session, we will be viewing a video that helps students understand what criminal and legal consequences you may face if you continue to bully.

- Are you going to stop bullying?

- How are you going to make up for the hurt you caused?

- Are you going to intervene or tell an adult when you see bullying?

Module #7: Victim of Constant Harassment and Bullying

Pause: Questions

- Do you now understand the difference between joking and bullying?

- Joking is when there is an even exchange and both parties truly think it is funny. It crosses the line into bullying when one of the parties feels badly, feels intimidated, or requests the other to stop.

- So, give me an example of joking and then give me an example of bullying.

- What is the difference between teasing, joking and bullying? **Answer:** teasing/joking becomes bullying when, 1) The victim of the joke reacts badly or sadly, 2) The victim asks the person joking to stop, or 3) The victim of the joke is not allowed to reciprocate the joke and is demeaned as a result of that situation. Provide an example such as Joey jokes *you walk funny and you look like an ape* to Tom. Tom becomes embarrassed and says nothing. Joey continues and starts making ape-like sounds around him. Same is true on line. When a victim of a joke is not allowed to have equal time to joke back or is demeaned in any way, it is bullying.

- Did you know that the number one reason children nine to fifteen years of age commit suicide is because they have been bullied and cannot take it anymore?

- At then end of our session, we will be viewing a video that helps students understand what criminal and legal consequences you may face if you continue to bully.

- Are you going to stop bullying?

- How are you going to make up for the hurt you caused?

- Are you going to intervene or tell an adult when you see bullying?

Module #8: Consequences and Criminal Charges a Bully May Face. This module should be viewed by every single child that has been found to bully and included with any other pertinent modules.

Pause: Questions

- In the state of Illinois, and other states, you can:
  - Be charged with a crime
  - You can be prosecuted and go through a trial
  - Your family can be sued
  - Your family can be forced to pay a large fine to either the state or the family and individual suing you. It could mean you lose things you love and enjoy doing because of the costs.
  - Do you understand what being charged with a crime means as well as what being sued means?

- Now that we know what it is, do you understand what can happen to you if you are found to be bullying?

- Do you understand bullying is abnormal and abhorrent behavior?

- Why is that true?

- Remind me of the difference between joking and bullying.

- Your behavior affects others and can seriously damage other students emotionally or physically.
- Do you understand that your bullying behavior can lead to:
    - The bullying behavior recorded in a permanent file that follows you through all schools, all the way to college
    - You can be charged with a crime
    - Your family can be sued

Bullying Incident Report Template

Middle School
BULLYING INCIDENT Report

Student's Name:_____ ID#_____ Grade_____ Today's Date_____

Date of Incident:_____ Time of incident:_____ Repeat infraction? ☐ Yes ☐ No

Cross-grade level? ☐ Yes ☐ No   Victim or Bully?_____

Check one: ☐Reported by teacher ☐ Reported by student   ☐ Reported by bystander

☐Reported by parent ☐ Reported by bus driver ☐ Other_____
Please indicate

Have the appropriate teachers/
staff been notified?   ☐ Yes ☐ No   Method of notification:_____

Type of Incident:

☐Verbal ☐Physical - Result in injury? ☐ Yes ☐ No   Reported to school nurse? ☐Yes ☐No

☐Debooking ☐Cyber(MySpace, Facebook, etc.)   ☐Other (Describe incident)

_____
_____
_____
_____

Location of incident   List all witnesses
(be specific):_____   (teachers/students):_____

Follow-up:

Remediation action(s):
   ☐ Conference with Student   ☐ Parent Notification   ☐ Social Worker Conference
   ☐ Counselor Conference   ☐ Police Notification   ☐ School Psychologist Conference
   ☐ Other

Consequence(s): ☐ Warning ☐ Detention(s)   ☐ Friday DT   ☐ ISS   ☐ OSS ☐ Police Referral
            ☐ Other

NOTES:

_____
_____
_____
_____

Follow-up Conference   **Date:**_____   **Time:** _____

Conducted by: _____

People present:

□ Administrator_____   □ Social Worker_____

□ Counselor_____   □ Teacher_____

□ Parent _____   □ Student _____

□ Witnesses _____

□ School Psych._____   □ Other _____

According to student, situation is: ☐ Better   ☐ Worse   ☐ No difference

Parent Contact: **Date:**_____   **Time:**_____

Person making contact: _____

Additional Actions / Notes:

_____
_____
_____

Follow-up Conference   **Date:**_____   **Time:** _____

Conducted by: _____

People present:

□ Administrator_____   □ Social Worker_____

□ Counselor_____   □ Teacher_____

□ Parent _____   □ Student _____

□ Witnesses _____

□ School Psych._____   □ Other _____

According to student, situation is: ☐ Better   ☐ Worse   ☐ No difference

Parent Contact: **Date:**_____   **Time:**_____

Person making contact: _____

Additional Actions / Notes:

_____
_____
_____

FAMILY CONTRACT TEMPLATE

The following is a contract that can be revised based on the specifics of any bullying situation. It can be implemented by the school, attorney or other neutral parties for those families involved

I. Acknowledgement and Purpose

1. Bullying is defined by state law [**and school policy**] as any severe or pervasive physical or verbal act or conduct (including written and electronic communications) directed toward a student or students, that has or can be reasonably predicted to have the effect of one or more of the following: placing the student or students in reasonable fear of harm to their person or property; causing a substantially detrimental effect on the student's or students' physical or mental health; substantially interfering with the student's or students' academic performance; or substantially interfering with the student's or students' ability to participate in or benefit from the services, activities, or privileges provided by a school.

2. Bullying includes: harassment, threats, intimidation, stalking, physical violence, sexual harassment, sexual violence, theft, public humiliation, destruction of property, or retaliation for asserting or alleging an act of bullying.

3. [**Offender**] and [**Offender's Parent(s)/Guardian(s)**] acknowledge that [**Offender**] has engaged in inappropriate conduct toward [**Victim**] that rises to the level of bullying, as defined above.

4. [**Offender's Parent(s)/Guardian(s)**] and [**Victim's Parent(s)/Guardian(s)**] wish to avoid further incidents of bullying, as well as further disciplinary or legal action due to [**Offender's**] bullying and therefore have come together to commit to take immediate action to stop any and all bullying of [**Victim**], or any other students.

5. [**Offender's Parent(s)/Guardian(s)**] and [**Victim's Parent(s)/Guardian(s)**] further commit to taking all steps necessary to create a positive environment for their children's personal growth and development and to ensure that all students feel safe and respected at school.

II. [Offender's] Commitment and Agreement

6. [**Offender**] acknowledges and understands that if he/she engages in further acts of bullying, he/she will be subject to further disciplinary action, including

suspension or expulsion from school, and could face criminal charges or a civil lawsuit.

7. [**Offender**] agrees and commits to (a) stop all bullying activity immediately and permanently, including online, in-person, or other media or electronic-based bullying; (b) only communicate with [**Victim**] if it is directly related to a school assignment, program, or activity; (c) never talk about [**Victim**] with other students; (d) treat all students with respect; (e) review and comply with the school's policies with regard to bullying, including reporting any acts of bullying committed by other students; and (f) keep this agreement and the discussions regarding this agreement confidential.

III. [Victim's] Commitment and Agreement

8. [**Victim**] agrees to (a) never talk about the Offender with other students; (b) treat all students with respect; (c) review and comply with the school's policies and support system with regard to bullying, including reporting any acts of bullying committed by other students; and (d) keep this agreement and the discussions regarding this agreement confidential.

IV. [Offender's Parent(s)/Guardian(s)] Commitment and Agreement

9. [**Name(s)**] agree to (a) encourage [**Offender**] to always respect others; (b) instruct [**Offender**] to immediately and permanently stop engaging in any acts of bullying and to take all necessary steps to ensure [**Offender**] does not engage in bullying toward [**Victim**] or anyone else; (c) instruct [**Offender**] to report any bullying to the school; (d) to report any bullying to the school; and (e) keep this contract and the discussions regarding this contract confidential, except as necessary to communicate with the school regarding the limitations on communications between [**Offender**] and [**Victim**].

V. The Victim's Parent(s)/Guardian(s) Commitment and Agreement

10. [**Names**] agree to (a) encourage [**Victim**] to always respect others; (b) to instruct [**Victim**] not to bully; and (c) instruct [**Victim**] to report and/or assist [**Victim**] in promptly reporting any bullying to the school; (c) keep this contract and the discussions regarding this contract confidential, except as necessary to communicate with the school regarding the limitations on communications between [**Offender**] and [**Victim**].

VI. Violations of this Agreement and the Anti-Bullying Commitment

11. If these commitments and agreements are violated, all parties consent and agree to promptly reconvene and meet with a group of professionals, including, but not limited to, school officials, law enforcement, and/or attorneys.

12. _____   _____
        [Offender]   Date

13. _____   _____
        [Victim]   Date

14. _____   _____
        [Offender's Parent(s)/Guardian(s)]   Date

    _____   _____
15. [Victim's Parent(s)/Guardian(s)]   Date

LESSONS LEARNED

- Just do it!

REFERENCES

American Heritage Dictionary, 2008

Guidance and support for cyber-bullied youth - www.Bullyonline.org

Bully Police USA - State-by-state anti-bullying laws and historical information on legislative activity - www.Bullypolice.org

Collaborative for Academic, Social and Emotional Learning - Organization dedicated to creating empathetic, team-oriented and successful learners throughout the U.S. education system - www.casel.org

National Bullying Summit, August 11-12, 2011 - Presented by the U.S. Secretary of Education.

National Education Association - www.nea.org

National Middle School Association - www.nmsa.org

The Gay, Lesbian and Straight Education Network - www.glsen.org

Waiting For Superman Documentary, Davis Guggenheim, 2010, nationally released documentary

U.S. Secretary of Education Offices - www.ed.gov

Guidance and research for parents and schools - www.howtostopbullying.com

Olweus Bullying Prevention Program. World-renown expert Dan Olweus provides methods and guidance for parents and schools - www.olweus.org

A support driven site designed to help parents, families and friends of lesbians and gays with resources, guidance and advice - www.pflag.org

Statistical information on bullying and its impact - www.safeyouth.org

Guidance and resources for schools to use in their facilities - www.schoolsantibullying.com

U.S. Government website with anti-bullying information - www.stopbullyingnow.hrsa.gov

The International Bullying Prevention Association - www.stopbullyingworld.org